W9-BFG-985

ONE TRUE DOCTRINE

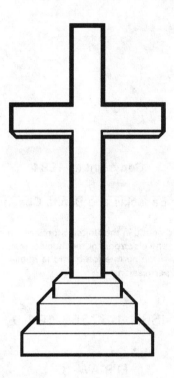

James Babeckis
&
Benita A. Chapman

Copyright © 1994
by
Jim Babeckis and Benita Chapman

All Rights Reserved. Printed and bound in the United States of America. No part of this book may be reproduced in any form or by any electronic or mechanical means including information storage and retrieval systems without written permission from the Publisher. Reviewers may quote brief passages to be printed without permission.

ISBN 1-57353-104-9

EPB-AW-104
an
ESCHATON BOOK
from

P R O D U C T I O N S ,   I N C .
60 East Chestnut Street, #236
Chicago, IL 60611

Dedication

It is not our purpose to convert anyone to any other religion. We want only to have you think, question and seek for the truth in whatever religion you choose to follow.

A favorite motto of ours is the one that states:
"There is no Religion higher than Truth"

We therefore dedicate this work to all who sincerely seek the truth for themselves and bother none along the way.

Contents

Preface

Is there one true doctrine, one universal religious truth? If there is, which religion, church or group can truthfully claim it as their own? If there is truly a Universal Truth upon which all religious truth rests, where it is today? And from where did it come? One also might inquire as to where it has gone for there is so much persecution and fighting amongst all people, even among the various Christian denominations as to led one to inquire about the sanity of all.

Today, still there is fighting between Catholics and Protestants, in Ireland. Both kill members of the opposite denomination with no guilt or repentance or at the least, very little or we assume the fighting would stop. This is not a matter of a "Foreign" Nation invading another country. Both groups have existed in Ireland since the early thirteenth century. Pope Adrian IV gave Henry II, then king of England, permission to occupy the island for the payment, to the church of Rome, of a yearly amount decided between the previous Pope and English monarch back in 1155 CE.

The Arabs and the Israelites still fight over Israel. The Crusades, a "holy war" were launched during the 1400's to drive the "Infidels" from the Holy Land.

Let us keep in mind that the mechanism of all "holy wars" is hate! Usually, church sponsored and church inspired hate. The targeting of specific groups within a country, whether heretics (non-believers), Jews, Communists, Feminists, or Homosexuals. The church perceives any opposition as the work of Satan. During World War II the Nazi's began wholesale extermination of the Jewish Race.

> "Christ was the greatest early fighter in the battle against the world
> enemy, the Jews... The work that Christ started but could not finish I
> ... will conclude." [1]
>
> - Adolph Hitler

Hitler's program of extermination was essentially a fundamentalist program because of its overriding moral characteristics. Hitler violently opposed "adultery", or any type of liberating ideas or policies concerning women, in this regard, he felt as many males still do today. Hitler opposed any role for women outside that of wife and mother. He was against abortion but this didn't prevent him from murdering innocent children or pregnant women. He was against pornography but created Auschwitz. What truth? What guiding principles are at work here? Let's leave the present and return to an earlier and simpler time. To find out what early man and his religions knew that we have seemingly lost.

We believe that in the beginning, man possessed true religious knowledge, understood the construction of the universe, the single eternal power that created it along with the laws that governed it. This is the explanation for the similarities found in the religions of various people widely separated in time and space. This information is being unearthed by archaeologists today, that early man sought to explain the forces that operated throughout the cosmos. Before the Gods of Olympus held sway, man knew or felt that the Sun, Moon and Stars were not Gods, merely outward manifestations of the eternal powers of the eternal life of the universe. However, overtime the abstractions proved too difficult for the common person to understand. In an attempt to simplify things for the multitudes, the heavenly bodies where personified.

The human (personified) figure came to be looked on as having actually lived and the truth became distorted and lost. What was a pure religion in one generation became mythology in the next and romance in the generations following. A secondary symbolism grew up around the first to further distort and hide the truth. It is the varied and often conflicting interpretation of the symbolism that led to the diversity of creeds and superstitions. This has made the world we know the battleground of war, cruelty and persecution that it has become.

> **"We are so engaged in doing things to achieve purposes of outer value that we forget that the inner all important rapture of being alive, is what its all about."[2]**
> - Campbell

Introduction

Where do we get the word for Bible and what does it mean? Let's give a little background on the historical meaning of the Bible.

The word Bible comes from the name of Byblos, the City of the Great Mother, who was known as Astarte, to the Greeks, the patron Goddess of learning. Her Priestesses collected a vast library of scrolls of holy works. After some time the Greeks began calling any papyrus byblos, for holy book. Hence our modern "holy book" or Bible.

St. Jerome, working during the 4th century, collected some Hebrew manuscripts and edited them to produce the Latin Vulgate. As we know now they were riddled with inaccuracies and differed greatly from his source texts.

The compilers of the King James Bible relied heavily on a Greek text edited by Erasmus in the 16th century, which itself was based on earlier Byzantine manuscripts assembled in Constantinople during the 4th to 8th centuries. There are no known fragments older than the 4th century.

The Revised Version of the New Testament attempted to correct deficiencies in earlier New Testaments and was published in 1881. It deleted the last twelve verses of the Gospel of Mark , which were known to be spurious and of a later date. It did away with the story of "Joseph and his mother" which had been written to preserve the virgin birth story. It included the forged interpretation intended to uphold the doctrine of the trinity: "For there are three that bear witness in heaven, the Father, the Word, and the Holy Ghost: and these three are one." This sentence cannot be found appearing anywhere until the 15th century. The Catholic Church insisted that the forgery be retained.

Until only recently, during the last hundred years or so, the Church discouraged any lay person from even reading the Bible. During the Middle Ages, anyone having an English translation of the Bible would be put to death.

In more modern times Dr. Baylee has said that the Bible is "infallibly accurate; all its histories and narrations of every kind are without any inaccuracy."

A Dr. Hodge is quoted as saying that all books of the Bible are "one and all, in thought and verbal expression, in substance, and in form, wholly the work of God, conveying with absolute accuracy and divine authority all that God meant to convey without human additions or admixtures."

A Catholic Theologian, Dr Alex Geddes, who translated the Old Testament as early as 1792 proved that the Pentateuch could not be the work of Moses or anyone prior to the time of David. He was denounced. As time marched on, it became increasingly difficult to support a position that the Scriptures were anything but a confused mass of myth, legend and garbled history. A book of Biblical essays published at this time gave up any pretence at authenticity for scriptures. There was of course an on-going resistance to scholarly efforts that were unraveling the foundations of Christianity. When the theologians began to give in they expressed a deep seated fear that viewing the Bible as myth would destroy their reputations, respect, and livelihood. After the mid 1800's the position of the historical authenticity and the Gospels as literal truth became no longer supportable.

"If the Christ-Myth theory is true, and if Jesus never lived, the whole civilized world has been living under the spell of a lie." was the thought of Rev. Maurice Jones. The Archbishop of Canterbury found it impossible to deny the Bible's apparent lies. What you have just read is a brief background of what the Bible has, already, during the 1700 and 1800's been proven to be. Most of this "history" is only known in scholarly circles and is not made known to the majority of Christians. It is, however, something that affects everyone in the Christian world. If no one has ever mentioned the truth of the Bible to you, you will find it in this book. Please read on.

The "bottom-line" here is that organized religions have a deep economic interest in maintaining the literal interpretation of the Bible myths.

*In this book we **do not** use the abbreviations BC for "Before Christ" as an indication of a period of time. We prefer instead to use BCE, which stands for "Before Christian Era". Likewise, we **do not** use the abbreviation AD for Anno Domini preferring instead CE for "Christian Era". We feel that these abbreviations are much more accurate for use in this book. Please be forewarned.*

"Every compromise of the truthfulness of the Bible must at the same time be regarded as a compromise of its authority."
- F. F. Bruce

Chapter One

The Bible As Guiding Principle

Most religions today reference the Bible to various degrees. Many have evening Bible study classes that parishioners may attend to become more familiar with the teachings presented and will relate these to everyday life to help people cope with the problems life presents to us all daily.

Many people across the land have given up being Methodists, or Lutherans, or Calvinists or Catholics and follow the Bible exclusively. They disagree with certain tenets of various denominations but believe that the Bible is the Word of God.

> Who actually wrote the Bible?
> Is it truly the word of God ?
> Is it dependable as a source of spiritual and moral teaching?
> Can we truly turn to the Bible for enlightenment?
> Can we use the Bible as a code of conduct for our daily lives?

These answers and more depend a great deal on our purpose in reading the Bible.

> "Our ultimate purpose in reading the Bible is to make us better men
> and women." [1]
>
> - Immanuel Kant

The Bible is published in over 286 different languages and sold in over 150 different countries. Although, less than one per-cent of the Japanese people claim Christianity as their religion they accounted for the purchase of one hundred and fifty million Bibles in the early nineteen eighties. [2]

In West Germany, the Bible is only outsold by atlases and cookbooks. According to available statistics, [3] out of one hundred Bible owners only fifteen people actually spend any time reading it, to the others it is something that they want to have in the home but assume that owning it is enough while to Fundamentalist readers; the Holy Bible is the literal embodiment of their faith and it probably wouldn't matter to them even if not one verse or line in a thousand could be corroborated by historical evidence. [4] The contents of the various books were brought together over a period of somewhere in the vicinity of 1500 years. The earliest writings date from about 1200 BCE. The books of the Old Testament in particular were handed down by word of mouth as oral tradition for generations before being committed to writing. The stories were those that were told around the campfires and most likely were slightly embellished with each telling. The original texts were not available to the scholars who wrote our modern day versions. The modern versions all derive from Latin translations of the earlier Hebrew and Greek texts. These Latin versions date from about 1000 CE.[5]

> "Therefore I speak to them in parables for seeing they see not and hearing they hear not, neither do they understand."
> ### Matthew 4:13

Before we try to answer any of the earlier questions, let's take a look at what books go into making up the Old Testament...

Old Testament Books

The Old Testament, in the King James version, which was our reference text, is composed of the following thirty-nine books:

Genesis	Ecclesiastes
Exodus	Song of Solomon
Leviticus	Isaiah
Numbers	Jeremiah
Deuteronomy	Lamentations
Joshua	Ezekiel
Judges	Daniel
Ruth	Hosiah
Samuel I	Joel
Samuel II	Amos
Kings I	Obadiah
Kings II	Jonah
Chronicles I	Micah
Chronicles II	Nahum
Ezra	Habakkuk
Nehemiah	Zephaniah
*	Haggai
Esther	Zechariah
Job	Malachi
Psalms	
Proverbs	

* Several other books that appeared in the Greek translation of the Old Testament - the Septuagint appeared also in the original edition of the King James Bible but were left out of later editions. The Book of Tobias follows Nehemiah in Catholic Versions of the Bible, The Book of Judith is found only in the Septuagint, the Hebrew "original", if it exists has yet to be found. Maccabees I & II appear only in the Catholic Bible, The New English Bible and The King James Apocrypha.

In the following pages, we will give you, dear reader, an insight into the Bible that we guarantee you will not get from any Bible study class. We will back up with proof; quotes, references and dates everything said so that those of you who wish to may discover for yourself the truth, the whole truth and nothing but the truth.

Let's return to examine the questions asked a moment ago -- The first question we asked before was who actually wrote the Bible. The Bible was not written by God. God does not author any writings of any kind. God does not have a mouth or arms or feet or hands. First off, the Bible was not written by saints or prophets or by "inspired" holy men. The Bible was written by power-hungry priests trying to convert the ignorant masses to Christianity. If you were trying to start a new religion in which men played the dominant role how would you start?

The rhetorician Lucian, born in Syria during the first century, circa 120 BCE, wrote about Christianity, a new religion at that time. He wrote that it was aimed at **"an unusually gullible class of people."**[6]

The earliest writers that took any notice of Christianity were Tacitus and Pliny. Both gentlemen thought of Christians as **"superstitious fanatics."** [7]

Sigmund Freud, the psychologist, states in one of his works his thoughts on the Bible:

> **"Biblical religion has the character of a neurosis, where a screen of mythical figures hides a repressed conviction of guilt, which it is felt, must be atoned, and yet cannot be consciously faced."**[8]

Some of the most brilliant thinkers of the early Christian era were the historians and authors from whom we've learned the most about the time in which they lived. Learned men like Porphyry, when speaking of Christianity called it **"blasphemy barbarously bold."**[9]

On the subject of Christianity, Tacitus says: **"It is a pernicious superstition."**[10]

"The new faith is a perverse and extravagant superstition." - Pliny. [11]

"A superstition vain and frantic." - Suetonius. [12]

The New Testament itself tell us the disciples were **"unlearned and ignorant men."** The Jewish judges before whom the unlearned and ignorant were brought called the Christians "idioti", from which our present day word idiot derives.

The Jewish Samaritans called the early Christians "Thartacs" and the period of the early church was described as the reign of Thartac. Thartac was the Egyptian god of credulity and vulgarness; he was portrayed as a man with a book, a cloak, and the head of an ass.

What these people perceived was that history had proceeded some distance, man and his intellect had made progress over the centuries. Greece was approaching a glory unknown in earlier times, Rome, a civilized grandeur. Whatever "evil" the early church suffered at the hands of its pagan neighbors, it was not, as the church eagerly states, because of any new gospel that it preached but because of the old absurdities that they resurrected in the name of religion combined with a belief in literal mythology. Concepts that Greece, Rome and the other civilized cultures had long ago abandoned. This was the "blasphemy" that Porphory wrote of.

Thomas Paine, one of the leaders of the American Revolution and Founding Fathers of our country, spent a good part of his adult life fighting the Bible, it's God, and it's ideas.

> **"Whenever we read the obscene stories, the debaucheries, the cruel and torturous executions, the unrelenting vindictiveness, with which more than half the Bible is filled, it would be more consistent that we called it the word of a demon than the work of God. It is a history of wickedness, that has served to corrupt and brutalize mankind; and for my part I sincerely detest it, as I detest everything that is cruel."** [13]
>
> - Paine

Thomas Jefferson, another of our Founding Fathers, thought that the teachings of Christ boiled down to a set of moral maxims. Everything else was **"priest-craft and superstition."** [14]

Let us go now to Genesis, the first book of the Bible, examine its roots and authenticity. In Genesis, we find the creation of the universe by a male God, but if we go back far enough in history we find that it is a Mother Goddess who gives birth to the universe. [15]

In the following story we see The Goddess as Universal Mother, but the myth shows signs of being tampered with even at this date. This myth comes from c. 600 BCE. Compare it with the earlier myth which follows it.

The Babylonian Epic of Marduk
(Sun God over the Goddess)
A Creation Story (c. 600 BCE)

Lahmu and Lahamu came into being and were called by their names. Even before they had matured and become full grown, Anshar and Keshar were created and surpassed them in stature. These lived many days, adding years to their days and their first born, heir presumptive, was Anu, the rival of his father, equaling Anshar. Ea was born of Anu, in his likeness, the master of his fathers, broad of understanding, greatly wise and mighty in strength, even stronger than Anshar, his Grandfather, with no rival among the Gods. His brothers and these divine beings, troubled and disturbed the inner peace of Tiamat, moving and running about within their divine home. This troubled Apsu greatly. He could not still them. Through it all Tiamat remained quiet even though she was in pain. Where Apsu, the begetter of the Gods, called his advisor, Mummu and said to him: "Mummu, who gives me joy and advice, let us go to Tiamat." So they journeyed and sat before Tiamat and discussed their first born. Apsu opened his mouth and said loudly to the glistening one, Tiamat: "Their behavior has become an annoyance to me, by day I cannot rest; by night I cannot sleep. I shall destroy them, putting an end to their behavior; and when silence is restored, let us sleep." But Tiamat hearing this became angry and pondering his evil in her heart cried out, "Why destroy what we ourselves have produced? Their behavior is indeed painful but let us take it in good will." Mummu counseled Apsu, not giving good advice, saying: "Yes father, put an end to their disorder and have rest by day and sleep by night." Upon hearing this Apsu brightened with an evil plan to destroy his progeny. But of what they planned in this way, the Gods found out and made haste. They took to silence, sitting quietly.

Ea drew a magic circle around the Gods and against the wicked plan of Apsu. Within the circle all took protection, and Ea composed a powerful spell which he recited over the water, out of which sleep poured down on Apsu and Apsu slept. After both Apsu and Mummu slept soundly, Ea loosened Apsu's tiara, carrying off his splendor which he put on for himself; returning to Apsu he slew him. On Apsu, he then built his dwelling place, and Mummu he seized holding him by a rope.

- This is not yet the end -- the myth is quite long and we will skip over parts of it. With this myth, however, we have arrived at the threshold of the psychology of both Freud and Rank as shown below.

* The Mythic malice of the Father.
* The love, even while in pain, of the Mother for her children.
* The rivalry of the siblings, Mammu as elder son, and Ea as young son, and finally a patricide with its mythically justified rational.

* **Essentially the myth is a complete reversal of all earlier formulas.**

* We see the ancient concept of Trinity, Apsu (Father), Tiamat (Mother Goddess), and Mummu (Son/Sun God).

* The pattern of biblical Genesis (creation) is seen here as well as the biblical "War between the Sons of Light and the Sons of Darkness."

* It is myth to set up the male gods as dominant over the female goddess.

* The pattern, also, is shown of a god, in the Bible Jehovah, in this myth Apsu, wanting and planning to destroy his creation, exactly what the Bible tells us God wanted to do. The seeds were planted here. The new male-oriented religion had to corrupt and retell the myths to "rationalize" their being.

The legend then proceeds to an account of the mounting fury of Tiamat with her son Ea, after discovering what he had done. The all mother Tiamat - "She who fashions all things" - gave birth to serpents, dragons, the great lion and the mad dog, the scorpion and various demons of storm. Eleven forms or monsters, she brought forth. After which she and her brood got ready for war, a battle with the Gods (all male, you will notice). Notice also, that the pattern of this myth was the same as used by the Greeks for their war of the titans with the Gods, which had the same purpose, the suppression of the Goddess in favor of the male god.

The conquest of a local matriarchal city, or group by invading patriarchal nomads is the reason. They reshaped local stories to serve their own ends. It is the employment of a priestly device still in use to this day, called by scholars, **mythological defamation**. As noted in "The Masks of God," it consists of terming the gods of vanquished people, demons and then inventing all sorts of secondary myths to illustrate the malice of the "demons" on one hand and the "majesty and righteousness of the god of the conqueror, on the other.

The similarities:

> Tiamat in this epic is similar to Tehom in Genesis 1:2.
>
> As Ea conquered Apsu, so did Yahweh the sea monsters (Job 26:12 13), and Leviathan (Job 4:1) (Psalm 74:14).

We are not saying that Biblical Genesis was taken from this story, only that the principals involved are the same. It is most likely that an earlier myth served as a basis for both stories.

The Mother of God (c. 1600 BCE)

I am She that is the natural Mother of all things, Mistress and Governess of all the elements, the initial progeny of Worlds, Chief of the Powers Divine, Queen of all that are in Hell, the Principal of them that dwell in Heaven, manifested alone and under one for of all the Gods and Goddesses. At my will the planets of the sky, the wholesome winds of the seas, and the lamentable silences of Hell are disposed; my name, my divinity is adored throughout the world, in the divers manners, in variable customs, and by many names.

For the Phrygians that are the first of all men call me the Mother of the Gods of Pessinuntica; the Athenians, which are sprung from their own soil, Minerva; the Cyprians, Venus; the Cretans, Diana; the Sicilians, Proserpine; the Eleusinians, their ancient Goddess, Ceres; some Juno, others Bellona, others Hecate, still others Ramnusie but to the Egyptians, who are accustomed to worship me and to call me by my true name, I am Queen Isis.

This legend shows, to some extent, the reverence paid to the "Mother of God" - the woman - and is from a time when everywhere throughout the near east the Goddess reigned supreme. The only male God was her son or lover, her consort. The male God had not yet usurped her as the ruler of Heaven. This translation is taken, not quite verbatim, from the Golden Ass of Apulius written several centuries BCE.

The biblical account that we are familiar with was a rewrite of the Babylonian creation myth which had the female goddess birthing the universe. There are other creation stories even older than the Babylonian, all of which feature a Mother Goddess. For example, the Hindu Creation myth is several thousand years older that the Hebrew one noted in the Bible.

Let us now examine the original sources for the remainder of the Old Testament.

Our purpose here is to list the Old Testament stories and give briefly one or two possible and earlier sources. We leave it up to you, the reader, if interested, to review the list of the original pagan sources from which the Bible was plagiarized.

Bible Story	**(Source)**
Genesis:	Babylonian
Adam & Eve:	Babylonian, Chaldean
Noah & Flood:	Babylonian, Chaldean

(There are in existence more than 400 flood stories, all which predate the Christian account. Most races or cultures have had similar myths to those found in the Bible, all share some points in common and all are far older than the Bible stories.)

Tower of Babel:	Akkadean, Sumerian
Abraham, Isaac & Jacob:	Babylonian, Hindu, Persian
Story of Joseph:	Egyptian (most likely)
Exodus:	Babylonian
Moses:	Egyptian, "Story of Sargon"
Ezekiel's vision:	Babylonian, Hindu, Orphic
Job:	Babylonian
Psalms:	Babylonian, Egyptian
Proverbs:	Various
Ecclesiastes:	Greek
King Solomon:	Egyptian, "Wisdom of Amenenomope"
Jonah:	Greek, Persian

The Old Testament

Chapter Two

The Old Testament

The Old Testament must be read, like any other piece of ancient literature, as a product, not of any god's literary talent, but of man's. A product of a very troubled time in history, not a product of eternity.

The books of Exodus, Leviticus, and Numbers supposedly derived from Moses were actually the product of a long development, brought from Babylon to Jerusalem by Ezra c. 400 BCE. The book had originally been commissioned by the Persian Emperor Artaxerxes as a book of rules for the people of Babylon.

The book of Deuteronomy was taken almost entirely from the "Book of the Law of Moses" allegedly found in Solomon's Temple by the priest Hilkiah (c.621 BCE). On the basis of this "find", the Old Testament was completely rewritten.[1] Until 621 BCE, no one had ever heard of this book.

Philo-Judaeus (20 BCE - 54 CE)
A devout Jew, began the task that he had assigned for himself. The task of reshaping Platonic and Stoic teaching to the pattern of Hebrew belief and tradition.

During the Middle Ages an attempt was made by a Jewish Philosopher known as Moses Maimonides (1135-1204 CE) to make Aristotle's writings compatible with Biblical Religion. His proofs for the existence of God were those of Aristotle. His concept of God was Neoplatonic. Although he was a devout Jew and was mainly concerned with saving the principles and thoughts of Judaism, he often deviated far from Judaism in spirit.

Origen (c. 254 CE)
Employed a corps of stenographers and copyists for twenty years collating the Hebrew text of the Old Testament, a Greek translation, and commentaries. He undertook to demonstrate all Christian dogmas from Old Testament and Pagan writings. We know this from his own works.

"Archaeology has unearthed the Old Testament's literary predecessors and thus disproved the idea that the Old Testament is a unique, unprecedented, and unified expression of God's word." [2]

- Barthel

"In older mythologies, the God enters the world voluntarily, as in a dance or play. It's joyous, humorous at least. There is no more dreary mythology than that of the Old Testament." [3]

- Campbell

Biblical Sources

"The legends of Creation, of the Garden of Eden, of the Flood, etc. were disengaged (stolen) from the grosser elements of Babylonian Mythology and were recast in the mold of the advancing religion of Israel." [4]

- Samuel S. Cohon,
Professor of Jewish Theology
Hebrew Union College

Adam & Eve

"A tale fit only for the ears of old women" [5]

- Celsus

There is nothing in the Bible, either Christian or Hebrew that cannot be found in the literature of older races. The first two chapters of Genesis present us with two separate and mutually contradictory accounts of Creation. The second creation story is a great deal older than the first. The first and later account is from c. 600 BCE, while the oldest and second account is c. 900 BCE.

And God said "Let us make man in our image, after our likeness: and let them have dominion over the cattle and over all the earth, and over every creeping thing that creepeth on the earth."
Genesis 1:26, 27

So God created man in his own image, in the image of God created he him; male and female created he them. And again in **Genesis 2:7**...

And the Lord God formed man of the dust of the ground, and breathed into his nostrils the breath of life; and man became a living soul.

14

Let's spend some time really looking at the Adam and Eve story in Genesis.

> "And out of the ground made the Lord God to grow every tree that is
> pleasant to the sight, and good for food; the tree of life also in the
> midst of the Garden, and the tree of the knowledge of good and evil."
>
> **Genesis 2:9**

There is no "real" physical tree of life as there is no real physical tree of good and evil.
This has to refer to something symbolic. The whole story is symbolic. Every culture
of the ancient world had some kind of creation story featuring a tree of life. In Greece,
it was Gogard, in Norse mythology the tree of life was the "world" tree Yggdrasil, to the
Hindus it was Ashvatta, among the Tibetans, the tree of life was called Zampun, to the
Persians, it was Homa. Even the Chinese had a tree story. In their story, the tree was
called Sung-Ming-Shu.

> "And a river went out of Eden to water the garden; and from thence it
> was parted, and became into four heads."
>
> **Genesis 2:10**

Again, read mythology books. Like everything else in the Bible this too is borrowed.
The Brahmin mythology speaks of four primeval rivers flowing from Mount Meru. In
Buddhist literature, four sacred rivers flow from the abode of Sikia, god of life. In the
Eden of Norse mythology known as Asgard, we again find four rivers. There is nothing
original anywhere in the Bible, much less in Genesis. It's all Cosmology.

In the Babylonian Gilgamesh epic written between c. 2,000 BCE we read:

> "Aruru washed her hands;
> Clay she pinched off and spat upon it;
> Eaboni, a hero she created,
> An exalted offspring with the might of Ninih." [6]

In other myths that explain creation, we have Hathor or Nut in Egypt, Nammu or
Ninhursag in Sumer, Tiamat and Mami in other parts of Mesopotamia.

The story of Adam & Eve also appears in the mythology of the Chaldean Scriptures
where the first man is known as Adam Adami. Also much older than the Hebrew story,
is the Hindu myth which was written c. 2,000 years BCE. It uses the same language,
and from all appearances, was the original. In the Hindu story, Adama & Heva are the
names of the first man and woman. The word *paradise* is from a Persian word meaning
garden and never occurs in the Old Testament. The word *Eden* was originally Sumerian
and meant "plain". An earlier version of this story features the Garden of the

Hesperides, who were the daughters of Atlas and Nix. Atlas was sentenced to keep watch over the golden apples in his daughters' garden, hence Eve is shown with an apple. To overcome Atlas and steal three of the apples is the first of the labors of Hercules.

If Adam and Eve weren't real, they didn't sin - hence there is no original sin to atone for!

The authors of Genesis were copying a myth of the harmony and beauty of the earth not a travelogue. Unable to grasp the myths allegorical meaning, Iraneus (c.130 CE), presented the Gnostic doctrine of the "atonement for sin" as the Original Sin of Adam. If this much of the Bible is false, what do you think the rest is?

> **Placing the blame for Adam's sins on his descendants was: "Exceedingly cruel and plainly inconsistent with the justice, wisdom, and goodness of our gracious God."**
>
> - Daniel Whitby, Rector
> Salisbury Cathedral (1710)

Nowhere on earth in any of the kingdoms of which science is aware, from the lowest insect up to and including man ("made in the image of God") does the male of the species ever, under any circumstances give birth or create life. This is a biological impossibility contrary to all laws of nature. Yet so many thousands even millions of people accept the Bible account of Eve coming from Adam's rib without blinking. Wake up and smell the coffee, people! When the male god concept was first introduced, it must have been very difficult explaining how "HE" could be the giver of life to all creation; man cannot produce either a child or food for the child from his own body. The whole attitude of humanity had to be changed drastically. This was done and through the greatest violence as is shown in the Old Testament.

> "And He said unto them, Thus saith the Lord God of Israel, put every
> man his sword by his side, and go in and out from gate to gate
> throughout the camp (city?), and slay every man his brother, and every

man his companion, and every man his neighbor. And the children (tribe) of Levy did according to the word of Moses: and there fell of the people that day about three thousand men."

Exodus 32:27,28

"So they smote him, and his sons, and all his people, until there was none left alive: and they possessed his land."

Numbers 21:35

"And we took all his cities at that time, and utterly destroyed the men, and the women, and the little ones, of every city, we left none to remain."

Deuteronomy 2:34

"And when the Lord thy God shall deliver them before thee; thou shalt smite them and utterly destroy them; thou shalt make no covenant with them; nor show mercy unto them."

Deuteronomy 7:2

"So Joshua smote all the country of the hills, and of the south, and of the vale, and of the springs, and all their kings: he left none remaining, but utterly destroyed all that breathed, as the Lord God of Israel commanded."

Joshua 10:40

"And the Lord sent thee on a journey, and said 'Go and utterly destroy the sinners the Amalekites, and fight against them until they be consumed'."

1 Samuel 15:18

"They, and all that appertained to them, went down alive into the pit, and the earth closed upon them: and they perished from among the congregation." (for reverting to paganism)

Numbers 16:49

Entire towns and villages wiped out wherever the Hebrew tribes took their new male god. These are only a few, there are many others, to numerous to list. The entire Old Testament is a chronicle of the new male God of the Hebrews versus the Goddess of the people in the lands they entered.

Whenever you encounter a story, biblical or otherwise, where it is so absurd and contradictory to nature as male gods brooding upon the waters or laying eggs (i.e. giving birth) then you know that you are reading an older goddess myth that has been rewritten by patriarchal scribes.

17

Every ancient race had this story, and some type of fruit is usually the temptation symbol. In Greece, it was an apple; in India it was figs.

Professor Chiera in his work "They Wrote on Clay" published in 1938 points out that "The Bible does not give us one creation story but several of them." Many other authors and biblical scholars are of similar opinion.

> The Bible is a collection of myths. The one featured in Chapter I, Genesis seems to be the one which had "the least vogue among the common people"[7] of the time in which it was written.
>
> - Chiera

> "The modern interpretation of the Bible, for example, starts with the premise that everything in the Book of Genesis up to the construction of the Tower of Babel is quite simply a parable in which the authors were trying to make comprehensible the unfathomable workings of the Lord."[8]
>
> - Barthel

Since most people never read any other accounts of creation, they assume there are no others. Keep in mind that the priests who wrote the Bible were not intending to reveal truth but to lay the basis for a male dominant religion.

> "The prophets persistently demanded of their people that they put their confidence in the superiority of their God, with whom their fortunes were bound up, over all other deities, and then strove to create reasons for their claims."[9]
>
> - Cohon

The Serpent in the Garden

Before the present Bible story of Adam, Eve and the Serpent, in which the serpent turns into something synonymous with evil and Satan, serpents were revered. Everywhere in myth and imagery the Goddess was pictured with her sacred serpent. In the Egyptian pictographic language the symbol for a cobra precedes the names of all Goddesses. In Australia, Venezuela, and the ancient middle east the distribution of the Goddess with her serpent was global.

The serpent was a symbol of eternal life since it was seen to shed its skin and renew itself. It was the symbol for rebirth. The serpent was also linked, in the ancient mind, with wisdom. In Greece, the oracle consulted by Kings, Princes and Philosophers alike were a Python Goddess. Sacred snakes kept at the Goddess's shrines were perhaps not

18

merely the symbols but actually the instrument through which the experience of divine revelation was reached.

The serpent coiled with its tail in its mouth formed the perfect circle, the cycle of all and of nothing.

In ancient Egypt, the symbol of the creation was a snake encircling a water vase. The snake was breathing on the waters, and its breath, impregnating the water, brings forth life and matter.

In the Mayan cosmology we have a seven headed serpent called Naga guarding its eggs -- the germinal life force.

In the Orient, we find the same seven headed serpent called Narayana, "The Mover on the Waters." The name of these waters was Amriti, which the Hebrews took for the name of Jonah's father.

In the Buddhist literature the serpent is again called Naga, identical to that of the Mayans in America. The seeds of "One True Doctrine?"

The Catholic Church tells us that St. Patrick drove the snakes from Ireland, as he surely did. In bringing the "Light" of Christianity, he drove out the symbolic Druid serpent and its wisdom. Scientists tell us there never were any snakes in Ireland.

Actually there is a historical explanation based on the coming of the Hebrews into Canaan and their subjugation of the inhabitants of Canaan. The principle deity of the people of Canaan was the Goddess, as she was everywhere before the coming of the Hebrews.

> "Accumulating archeological evidence affirms overwhelmingly that pre-
> historic peoples worshipped a female deity. This evidence and the
> earliest writings document the persistence of a Goddess religion for
> nearly thirty thousand years, beginning in the late Paleolithic."[10]
> - Gadon

Associated with the Goddess is the serpent, symbol of the mystery of life. The Male God oriented group rejected it. **There is a historical rejection of the mother implied in the Garden of Eden.**

As proofs that the serpent was not originally associated with evil we offer the following passages that appear to us to not have been changed by Bible copyists.

The Midianites were known as wise men, and called "sons of serpents", The Canaanites and Hamites also.

19

Such was the wisdom of the Midianites that Moses sought the advice and council of Hobab, the son of Raguel, the Midianite.

Numbers 10:29-31

The brazen serpent of Moses was worshipped by the Israelites as a god.

2 Kings 18:4

Compare Exodus (32:26-29) with Numbers (21:5-9).

The names of Heva, Hivi, Hevite, and Levi all signify a serpent.

The Levites (tribe of Levi) are always associated with the temple and is the tribe from which the Jewish priests were chosen.

Cain and Abel

This story is another Adam and Eve myth. This is a separate creation myth appended to the one found in Genesis. "Instead of sons of Adam & Eve, these two are Adam and Eve all over again." [11] All you have to do is compare them to see this.

Adam is alone and lonely, and so is Cain. Adam takes himself a wife and so does Cain. Adam sins, and so does Cain. Adam is banished, and so is Cain. Adam's land is cursed and so is Cain's. Adam is sent out to till the ground, and Cain is called a tiller of the ground. Adam goes to sleep and Cain goes to the "Land of Nod," a synonym for sleep. Adam's garden is eastward in Eden and Cain's city is on the east of Eden. Adam's wife is made subject to Adam and Cain's weaker brother Abel is made subject to Cain. Compare Genesis 4:7 with the words of God to Eve in Genesis 3:16. It's the same (or a similar) story.

Cain's descendants: Tubalcain and Jubal are the Hebrew equivalents of the Greek Gods Vulcan, the smith, and Orpheus, the musician.

The Bible story is a copy of the Persian myth of Ahriman and Ahura Mazda, who sacrificed to an elder god named Vayu. Ahriman became a traitor and eventually a devil after his sacrifice was found unacceptable by Vayu. The myth of Cain is based on primitive sacrificial magic. God is said to have placed a mark on Cain and anyone that killed him would be punished. Who could possibly kill him? No one else existed at this point, at least according to Genesis. The "mark" of Cain was originally the mark of a priest class so that all people would know them. Those who were entitled to sacrifice to the gods for the people. This again was corrupted in the Biblical retelling of Cain. If you know the story you'll know that it reflects the Hebrew hostility to an agricultural / matriarchal religion.

20

Noah and the Flood

All in all there are some 400 flood myths. Each with its Noah and the Ark.

> "And he went into the ark with his sons, and his wife, and his wife's sons, before the waters of the flood. 'All that I had, I caused to be put on board, the seed of many kinds of living creatures. I brought into the ship my family and all my kindred, herds and flocks of the fields, wild beasts of the fields. . ." [12]
>
> from the Epic of Gilgamesh
> (c. 2500 BCE)

> "In seven days all creatures who have offended me shall be destroyed by a deluge, but thou shalt be secured in a vessel miraculously formed; take therefor... and with seven holy men, your respective wives, and pairs of all animals. Enter the ark without fear; then shalt thou know God face to face, and all thy questions shall be answered." [13]
>
> from the Bhagavad-Gita
> (c.500 BCE)

This story is intended to be a myth. We don't feel that the author of "Noah" ever expected it to be taken literally as you will have to admit once we examine it a little.
The story of Noah begins with Genesis 6:6. A description of the Ark's size and construction is in Genesis 6:14. No one really agrees what on length a cubit actually was in biblical times. If we assume, as some do, that the cubit is only 18 inches, the Ark would not be very large. Some estimates place the biblical cubit at 20 inches. If we use the larger measurement, the length of the Ark would only be 500 feet. It would have a height of 83.3 feet and be 50 feet across. Into this, Noah put eight people, two of every kind of animal and food for all for 150 days. Other accounts say 7 of every animal and food for a period of one year.

The Ark is 500' long, 83.3' high and only has one small (1 cubit wide) window for ventilation. Now depending on the placement of the window and the animals, you could end up 250' from the only window. It being only 20 inches wide amidst all sorts of animals to whom, lest we forget, you are also considered food. A little preposterous? A little absurd? Have we suspended all reason and good common sense? Did Noah go to the North Pole for polar bears or to Australia for kangaroos? If there was a flood, what happened to the fish? They had a field day. Don't you think this might be allegory?

> "Even Jews view the narratives of the Bible as allegories with ethical, psychological, and philosophical content." [14]

Noah's three sons are given as Shem, Ham, and Japeth. In the Hindu version they are Sharma, Charma, and Jyapeti. Darn close.

And then the waters resided and the Ark comes to rest on Mt. Ararat. In the Babylonian story, it comes to rest on Mount Nisir. The Hindu story has the Ark coming to rest on Mount Himilaya, and in the Greek flood the Ark rests on Mount Parnassus.

After the flood, as a promise that never again would the Earth undergo such a deluge, the Goddess Ishtar, the Lady of the Rainbow, hung out her multicolored necklace. This story like all the others in the Bible, was copied from earlier Pagan sources.

> **"It is believable precisely because it is absurd"** [15]
>
> **- Tertullian**

The Tower of Babel

The Tower of Babel illustrates the Hebrew concept that Hebrew is the language of God and all other languages are secondary.

Genesis 11:6-7 And the Lord said, behold, the people are one, and they all have one language; and this they begin to do; and now nothing will be restrained from them. The "Tower of Babel" is actually the last of the creation stories found in the Old Testament.

This myth is found all over the world including India and Mexico. It was familiar in Greece where giants piled high mountains to reach heaven. Hindus said it was not a tower or mountains but a tree that grew to heaven and angered Brahma who cut off the branches and threw them down. All the myths share common aspects that include an explanation for the diversity of languages. Even in the Western Hemisphere we find the very same myth among the Choctaw Indians who say their ancestors piled up stones to build a mountain to reach up to heaven. In Central America we find a story of a pyramid built by giants but the angry gods shattered it with lightning.

Abraham, Isaac, and Jacob

In **Genesis 12:7** Abram received God's blessing and promise that at the age of seventy-five , he would have children, but his wife did not bear his son till twenty-five years later when Abram was one hundred years old.

In **Genesis 12:10-20** Abram lied to the Egyptians by telling them that his wife Sarai was his sister. The pharaoh gave Abram many gifts including sheep, oxen, he asses, and menservants, maidservants, she asses and camels as dowry and took Sarai as his wife. However real this may sound we know that **camels weren't domesticated until the late**

22

thirteenth century BCE. This is at least two hundred years too late for Abraham to have owned one.

God plagued pharaoh and his house. Why? Pharaoh acted in good faith, it wasn't his fault that Abram lied to him.

God promised Abram, later to become Abraham, in **Genesis 17:5** three times that if he did as God instructed him, he would be given a son who would become a leader of a great nation. When this son became older, God commanded Abraham to take his only son and to make of him a burnt offering to God. The Bible claims that God was testing Abraham's loyalty. Isn't this cruel and unusual for one of God's favored? It would be if it had actually happened.

In his Epistle to the Galatians (**Galatians 4:24**), the apostle Paul asserts that this whole story is an allegory.

The Story of Joseph
(A tale of Two Brothers)

Joseph's brothers throw him into a pit because of their jealousy. This is another retelling of the Genesis Creation story. It is the story of God casting Satan out of heaven into the fiery pit or hell. The myths in the Bible are told and retold over and over again. The copyists never read what they are copying or else attributed more intelligence to future generations than they should have. A multicolored vestment was the mark of the well known wizard-priests of Babylon and probably explains the coat of many colors worn by Joseph.

Moses (Exodus)

To most people, Moses is a historical figure. The truth is that Moses is a myth like everything else we read in the Bible. The story of Moses was taken from the Egyptian account which is dated 2,000 years earlier than the Hebrew Bible story. The Hebrews spent many years in captivity in Egypt and had ready access to its myths and secrets. Moses's flowering rod, his plague on Egypt of a river of blood, the tablets of the law brought down from the mountain top were all ancient goddess symbols. His miracle of drawing water from a rock was first done by the mother of the Greek god Zeus. It is also recorded in mythology of Atalanta and Artemis. His miracle of drying the Red Sea was first done by Isis.

Story of Sargon
(2350 BCE)

Sargon was born of a humble mother in the upper reaches of the Tigress. She put him in a little basket of rushes, made water tight by coating it with pitch. She placed him in the waters of the river. Sargon floated down river and was pulled out by a gardener on the royal estate. The Goddess so loved him that he advanced in rank and presently became ruler himself. Arabia, Assyria and Phoenicia all had their 'Moses' stories. They also had rods that became serpents. They too divided rivers.[16]

In like manner Perseas of the Greeks was shut up in a chest and cast into the sea, as was Osiris in a coffin placed in the Nile.

In his first Epistle to the Corinthians, Paul, the Apostle, states that Moses is only a story. (**Cor. 10:11**) Has no one ever read Paul to know this?

Book of Job

"Job demonstrates not only the illusory character of the orthodox Jewish view but also its utter uncharitableness."[17]

The Jewish Talmud states "Job was not created, but is an allegory."

There is a Babylonian poem that expresses the story and like much else of Biblical literature, is apparently the source:

"Into my prison, my house is turned,
Into the fetters of myself, my feet have stumbled,
With a whip he has beaten me;
All day long the pursuer pursues me
In the night watches he lets me suffer;
Through torture my joints are torn asunder;
My limbs are destroyed;
My sickness baffles the conjurers,
And the seer left dark my omens."[18]

Psalms

"Thou alone hast created the world according to thy wishes, with men and their herds and flocks, together with all wild creatures that are on the earth and that go upon the rivers and that soar through the air above us on their wings. How splendid are all the works of thy mind, Thou

Lord of Eternity. On earth all things are accomplished at a nod of thy head, for Thou art the Creator. Thou alone art life, for man lives but through Thee."

Beautiful isn't it? But it's not a psalm, it's the Hymn to The Sun written by the Pharaoh Akhenaten about 1330 BCE. [19]

The scribes that wrote the Old Testament had no qualms about borrowing from other cultures and religions. The entire Old Testament is plagiarized from Pagan sources.

Proverbs (c. 400 BCE)

"The product of many minds and many ages." [20]
- Barthel

The Book of Proverbs is attributed to King Solomon but is actually a collection of the common sense sayings of many cultures throughout the entire area of the ancient near East.

Ecclesiastes (c. 200 BCE)

"The author's weakened religious fervor probably reflects the influence of Greek skepticism. The author knows nothing of the judgement of the soul after death or of a resurrection." [21]
- Cohon

Scholars are pretty much agreed that Ecclesiastes could not have been written by Solomon or any of his contemporaries. The intense pessimism more strongly reflects the philosophical outlook of the Hellenistic era and was probably not written before 250 BCE.

Solomon
(The Wisdom of Amenenomope, c. 1000 BCE)

This is another creation myth. Samson, Samuel, Saul(Sol), and Solomon are all solar creation myths rewritten to reflect Hebrew thought and religious ideas.

Sol-Om-On are all names of the sun from different cultures. The entire book of judges (as is the whole of the Bible) is mythology. This book describes the suns journey through the zodiac.

Proverbs 8:23-30 tells us "I was set up from everlasting, from the beginning, before ever the earth was." Supposedly this proverb is referring to Solomon, but how could he have existed "before ever the earth was"? The sun could have though and did exist before our other planets came into being.

Jonah

The story of Jonah is another captivity myth. If you use a little common sense, you would realize no one could survive for three days in the belly of a fish. Why not believe in Mother Goose? Actually the story has been altered from an older existing "Bible" where we find Jonah emerging after three days from the "womb" of the whale. This is an old tale of a Pagan god, most likely Ea or Dagon being born to help mankind. It was "Christianized" and its true meaning obscured by the Bible copyists.

This too is not an original myth. There is, in Hindu mythology a story of Candragomin, who endangered a ship because a rival magician caused a storm and assumed the form of a fish to swallow him.

The Bible doesn't mention the name or the fish. There is a story in the Hebrew Kabbalah about Jonah. In this story, the fish is called Cetus, a latinized form of Dagon. In temples of Dagon (the Fish God) was a large male figure with the head of a fish. Inside the statue was a cell for prisoners. It is also possible that the story is about someone imprisoned in a statue of Dagon.

The entire Old Testament is nothing more than the documentation of the thousand year struggle between the new, male religion of the Hebrews with the earlier preexisting Goddess faith. The Hebrews were attempting to establish the male supremacy for the twelve tribes of Judah over the matriarchal religions and populations of the lands into which they moved.

Why would a god supposedly rational and benevolent, reveal to only one very primitive and backward nation, mysteries not accessible to the rest of humanity when he stated his purpose was to save all of us? This is not consistent and totally unworthy of any god.

Commentary I

The compilers of the Bible mixed and confused the writings of different authors with each other, which, even if we could find no other reasons, would alone be enough to destroy the authenticity of the Bible.

In the book of Isaiah, chapters 44 and 45 could have only been written by someone who lived at least 150 years after Isaiah. These chapters refer to Cyrus, king of Babylon, who permitted the Jews to return to Jerusalem from Babylon, to rebuild the temple.

Isaiah, according to biblical chronology, died 693 years before Christ. The decree of Cyrus, freeing the Jews, occurred 536 years before Christ or 162 years after Isaiah had died!

The Book of Jeremiah

This book has all the appearance of being a collection of unconnected stories, put together without date, order, or explanation. It is so disjointed that it cannot have been written at one time, by one writer, it gives every evidence of being hastily thrown together by several people at different times without reference to one anothers works. Several chapters narrate the same events but in a different style from one another and start over with the same thought expressed chapters before. A story is begun in 21:12-15 that is not completed until 16 chapters later (38:1).

Ezekiel and Daniel

Unlike the previous books, there is no internal evidence that tells us for certain that these two books are forgeries and not written by the persons whose names they bear. Because these two books were both written at the time that the Babylonian captivity began gives us good reason to believe that, at least, most of the books of the Bible were written during that time. These two books also differ from the other books of the Bible in content. They contain accounts of dreams and visions. Seeing that the Jews were in captivity gives us reason to believe that they could not speak freely and openly about all subjects. It would not be safe to openly express plans of escape. Information would need to be hidden or couched in terms that the intended recipients would understand but not others who might overhear or steal a message. It would be reasonable to suppose that the content of the dreams and visions spoken of in these books had to do with the return of the Jews to their own land and the deliverance from Babylon. This and nothing more. Today's romantic interpretations show how far the Christian "scholars" will go to explain the meaningless.

The New Testament

Chapter Three

The New Testament

In the King James version, we find the following twenty-five books:

Matthew	Thessalonians II
Mark	Timothy I
Luke	Timothy II
John	Titus
Acts	Philemon
Romans	Hebrews
Corinthians I	Peter I
Galatians	Peter II
Ephesians	John I
Philippians	John II
Colossians	John III
Thessalonians I	Jude
Revelation	

The Gospels

Those who study the Bible cannot say for sure if the Four Gospels are the work of four men or many men writing over a period of time. The evidence, however, points to the latter. The men who wrote what became known as the Gospels were not interested in writing an accurate, historical account of Christ. They couldn't do this, there was no historical Christ. They were creating a document to re-affirm the faith of the members of the various congregations of the early church.

In or about the year 350 CE, the individuals then forming the church began to form their hierarchy and to decide from all the bits and pieces of "sacred" writings in their possession which to make "doctrine" and which to exclude. The vote was taken and "The New Testament" came into being. The men of the church hierarchy decided by vote what would become the "word of God" and what would not.

The books of the New Testament were denied as forgeries at the time they were voted on as New Testament material.

About the year four hundred CE, Faust wrote that the books of the Evangelists had been composed long after the time of the apostles by obscure men, who (fearing that no one would believe them) published their beliefs under the names of the apostles. Faust went on to address himself to these obscure authors and called their writings "vague reports" and the writers "half Jews". [1]

The Manicheans, (a Christian Sect, later condemned as a heresy), rejected as false all of the New Testament, claiming to have other writings that were authentic. [2]

The Nazarenes rejected all of the Epistles of Paul and regarded him as an impostor.

It was common knowledge since the earliest days of the church, that the gospels were not originals.

The Bishop of Tunis complained in 506 CE that the gospels were being extensively changed in his day because they were written by "idiot evangelists" and needed correction. [3]

The Gospel according to Matthew is acknowledged to be derived from an earlier work known as "The Loggia of Matthew."

The title "Gospel according to ..." means "thought to be by ..." and not any one specific author. The interpreters evade the issue of eyewitness authority this way. Even the early church fathers wrote that they had not seen the originals.

The Book of Revelation was regarded as a forgery in 340 CE but included later.

Lacantius and other historians writing in the 4th century claimed that the Christians habitually lied about their books and copied other authors' material.

The philosopher Celsus, who lived around the second century knew the literature of the Church for what it really was. What Christians today consider time-tested doctrines, were to him, in his time, "missionary literature" and "propaganda". In his little-known work "On The True Doctrine", Celsus has much to say about Christian teachings.

We must consider that someone writing from the First and Second Centuries was closer to the origins of Christianity that we are in our day and age. What did Celsus know that we don't when he says "Let's speak about their systematic corruption of the truth, their misunderstanding of some fairly simple philosophic principles - which, of course, they completely botch."? If you keep in mind that all Christian doctrines are derived (read: plagiarized) from the earlier Pagan doctrines. You will see what Celsus knew and was

32

opposing. Celsus also tells us "Not only do they misunderstand the words of the philosophers; they even stoop to assigning words of the philosophers to their Jesus." [4]

Several of the sayings of Christ have been traced to Plato, who stated them much more eloquently. [5]

In 1263 CE, at the insistence of Urban IV, Thomas Aquinas began the laborious work of translating the works of Aristotle from the Greek. The results of these translations were his voluminous "Commentaries" that turned a potentially hostile Aristotle into an ally of Christian thought and made possible an assimilation of Aristotelian ideas into Christianity.

Christ Foretold

Christian Theologians like to tell us that Christ was prophesied. That we were told in the earliest Pagan literature that he was coming. We don't feel this is actually true. Many Gods have been "foretold" and there are similarities between Christ and several others. Rather than proving Christ's uniqueness, we think this proves the opposite. Christ is just another myth of a vegetation deity that was adapted by the Christians. We say "adapted" rather than "created" because created would imply something new. There are too many similarities between the Christ Myth and others to make him new. The myth of Christ had been foreshadowed 500 years before the arrival of Christianity by the Tragedy of Aeschylus entitled "Prometheus Bound". This is one of the reasons that the Church could not convert the Pagan population to Christianity. To them, Christ was just another vegetation god. Further, he was unknown to the learned historians and writers of the time he supposedly lived. Let us examine and compare Christ with the Prometheus myth.

Christ/Prometheus

1. Both perish on a hill.
2. Both submit to the will of another.
3. Both die to save mankind.
4. Both have their right sides pierced.
5. At the moment of their deaths, both express the same sentiments.

The Gospel writers repeat the words spoken by Prometheus five hundred years earlier, as Celsus has said they repeat the words of the Philosophers for Christ.

6. Both had a friend called Peter.
7. Both "Peters" deny their Gods.
8. Both Gods came to redeem mankind from sin.

Why do you believe in one and not the other?

The story (myth) of Christ shares aspects of many Gods and redeemers from Pagan mythology - **all who preceded him in time.**

The similarities between Christ and Prometheus are many, while the similarities between Christ and Krishna, of the Hindus, run into the hundreds.

You have only to read the whole story of Krishna to be impressed with the similarities without trying to number them.

What follows is a short list of Gods from various mythologies who underwent crucifixion to "redeem" their respective peoples.

Crucified Gods

1.	Christ	from	Nazareth
2.	Chrishna	from	India
3.	Sakia	from	India
4.	Indra	from	Tibet
5.	Mithras	from	Persia
6.	Tammuz	from	Babylon
7.	Criti	from	Chaldea
8.	Attis	from	Phrygia
9.	Odin	from	Scandinavia
10.	Hesus	of the	Druids

We only listed ten, we found references to sixteen, but why belabor the point? Christ was not unique among savior myths.

> **"The recurrent mythological event of the death and resurrection of a god, which had been for millenniums the central mystery of all the great religions of the Near East, became in Christian thought an event in time."** [6]

> - Campbell

The Virgin Birth

There are many virgin births written of in the literature of many nations.

The virgin birth wasn't selected as "doctrine" until the second century. St. Augustine was still denying it as late as the fifth century.

The Hebrews / Christians probably got their story from the Egyptian account where she was the lady Isis, Mother of Gods. There are many similarities between Mary, as Mother of Christ and Isis. There are similarities also, between Mary and Nari of the Hindus.

We know that Isis and her child Horus were the model for the images of Mary and child Jesus. Since the Hebrews spent much time in Egypt, could not the image of the Christian Mary not have had come from Egypt via the Hebrews.

The Bible tells us that Joseph was to have no part in the conception of the child. We are also told in the Bible that the child (Jesus) was to be of David's line. Joseph was of David's line but unless Mary was his sister or daughter, she could not be. Now, if Mary is not of David's line but has a child who is, we have to suspect that Joseph is the Holy Spirit spoken of by Luke. Food for thought.

On December 25th, the Persians celebrate the birth of their savior Zoroaster in a manger, in a cave and call him "The Ram of God who taketh away the sins of the World". Substitute 'Lamb' for 'Ram' and the similarity is apparent. Is this coincidence?

Still other Gods share the story: Apollo, Bacchus, Hermes, Mithra & Chrishna. All have similar births to virgins in caves or mangers.

It was not until the Fourth Century that the nativity was changed to December 25th. If Christ really lived and was born on a different date, how can the priesthood change it?

Another similarity related to the Virgin Birth. In Judea, it was Herod who wanted to destroy the baby Jesus. In the Egyptian myth, it was Herut who seeks to destroy Horus. At least half a dozen such stories exist that tell of infant heros and their narrow escapes from some form of destruction. Some you might want to read up on are: Hercules, Perseus, Alexander the Great, Romulus and Remus, and Horus mentioned above.

There are seventeen easy to find similarities between the titles of the Virgin Isis and Mary given in Blavatsky's works. Isis had women consecrated to her as does the Hindu Nari. The Christians gave Mary nuns consecrated to her as well.

Parents, Moms and Dads, May We have Your Attention Please: If you had a daughter, very young, engaged to be married, who walked in and told you one day, that she had been made pregnant by a ghost, but that it was OK because he was a holy ghost and an angel had told her it was going to happen ... what would you honestly think? You'd have her committed, we know you would, "for her own protection". Why then should we be asked to believe the same thing of another young girl, whom we never saw, told by no one knows for sure who, nor, for certain when, nor where and, of course, you believe it.

John the Baptist

A parallel story and by far older, comes to us from India where Ananda appears to be the model for John.

The similarities are:

Maha-Maya while pregnant with the Buddha visits Ananda's mother as Mary, pregnant with Jesus visited John's mother. The unborn children greet each other. We only need to compare the works of the Buddhists to find other similarities.

The rite of Baptism that John preached, appears in the temple legends of Sumeria. The Water God Ea of Sumeria was also called Oannes, which in Latin was Johannes, in Hebrew, Yohanan, and in English, John.

The story in the Bible could have come from either the Sumerian or the Hindu or might even have been a conscious or unconscious blending of both.

The Miracles of Christ

Do the miracles of Christ prove his divinity? Not really, if we look for stories from which the miracles derive. We find the Apostles attributed to Christ miracles recorded centuries earlier in India and originally attributed to Chrishna. It is very hard to find anything in the Gospels anywhere near approaching 'original'. The resurrection of the daughter of Jarius is a translation of the Hari-Purana attributed centuries before Christ to Chrishna.

The miracle of the multiplication of loaves and fishes took place in Bethany, in the Egyptian original it was Bethanu. The place of multiplying bread. Turning water into wine at marriage feast in Cana was copied from a Dionysian ritual practiced in many towns. Curing the blind with saliva was regularly done centuries before Christ by the Priestesses at Nineva.

The miracle of the raising of Lazarus occurs in the Egyptian scriptures also. Horus, the Egyptian savior journeys to Bethanu to raise his father. The names of Mary, Martha & Lazarus all come from Egypt. There are two sisters named Meri, and Merti, their 'brother' Lazarus is El-Azar-Us.

The Crucifixion

See previous list of crucified Gods. The cross, like every other Christian symbol, was 'borrowed' from Paganism. It did not occur until about 300 years after the event was alleged to have happened. The symbol of the cross with the body of Christ on it was not used until one hundred years later or four hundred years after the event was said to have happened.

History of the Cross [7]

The cross is the most ancient of symbols. It symbolizes the union of spirit and matter. In Astronomy, Mercury is the son of Corlus and Lux - of the sky and the light, or the sun; in mythology he is the son of Jupiter and Maia. He is the "Messenger" of his father, Jupiter, the Messiah of the sun; in Greek the name of Mercury is "Hermes", meaning among other things - "Interpreter", the word or logos. Mercury, besides being born on Mount Cyllene among shepherds, is the patron of shepherds. As a "messenger of the gods", he conducted souls of the dead to Hades and back again. Something that Jesus was supposed to have done. The symbols of Hermes - Mercury, were placed along and at intersections to the most traveled roadways and were cruciform.

Every seventh day the priest anointed these with oil, and once a year hung them with garlands, from which they came to be called "The Anointed". The word "christ" is the Greek translation of the Hebrew word which means "the anointed", the English translation of which means "Messiah".

The word "christ was most commonly used in the phrase "the Lord's christ". The translation of this is "the Lord's anointed one", in other words it was a reference to the king of the land not a savior. Mercury, when speaking through his oracles said, "I am he whom you call the Son of the Father, leaving the King of Heaven I come to help mortals". Mercury was known to heal the blind and restore sight.

"has every mark of fraud and imposition stamped upon it" [8]

- Thomas Paine

Many have invented similar tales to lead their simple minded hearers astray. Zamolxis, the servant of Pythagoras faked death and subsequent resurrection by hiding in a cave and convinced the Scythians that he had returned from the dead. Pythagoras himself did similarly, and there is a Rhampsinitus in Egypt who did likewise.

Rhamsinitus even claimed to have played dice with Demeter in Hades and brought back a golden napkin as proof.

Orpheus, Hercules and Theseus all are said also, in legends, to have gone to the Underworld and returned, thereby defeating death.

The episode of Christ's descent into Hell, found in the later Apostle's Creed, was added as an afterthought. It appeared only after the Sixth Century and was not included in any version prior to this time. It was and is, an interpolation copied from other fables and made an act of faith for all Catholics.

The Revelation of St. John

"The accidents of history have brought Paul to us in relative clarity but have left the apostle John in obscurity ..." [9]

As early as the fourth century, Eusebius noted that the scholars of his time doubted the authenticity of the Apocalypse.

The Revelation of St. John is from the Zoroastrian (Persia) struggle between Ahriman, who represents darkness and Ormazd, who represents Light. The myth is Persian but can be traced back even further to the Brahmins of India. The followers and priests of Zoroaster revolted and left India taking the mythology and God with them. It is a myth recorded by a scribe as "Revelation."

The present day belief that God is all good and Satan is evil is a direct descendant of the Zoroastrian myth. Is God off somewhere apart from Mankind or is the universe and everything in it a part of God? Can there be anyplace where God is not? If the universe is truly within the body of God then evil exists within God. Can the body of God be evil? If not, we need to readjust our thinking.

Commentary II

In the story of Herod, in order to kill the future king of the Jews, Herod decrees that all children under the age of two should be killed. Jesus escapes by accompanying Mary and Joseph to Egypt. John, the cousin of Jesus, who stayed behind, does as well as Jesus who supposedly left, for he wasn't killed by Herod. A small oversight on someone's part that costs this story its credibility.

A few other contradictions found are the following:

What are the apostles to do?

Mat. (10:10) : Jesus tells his followers to go and preach taking "neither" shoes and staves.

Mark (6:8-9) : Jesus tells his followers to go and preach taking "only" shoes and staves.

How many will be saved?

Luke (13:24) : says that many will seek to enter heaven and not be able. This is contradicted in Matthew.

Mat.(7:8) : says that "everyone" that asketh receiveth and he that seeketh findeth.

On Good Works

The prophets must have been very confused. **Mat (5:16) :** says to do good works openly. **Mat (6:1) :** says to do good works in secret.

The Ascension

The Ascension is ignored by two of the four New Testament writers. The two that do mention it disagree on its location, Mark says Jerusalem and Luke says Bethany. The Acts of the apostles contradicts both of them and agrees with neither.

The Sermon on the Mount

was delivered on a mount only according to Matthew: **Mat (5:1).** According to Luke, it was given on a plain **Luke (6:17).**

> "The New Testament compared with the Old is like a farce of one act."
>
> — Thomas Paine

Chapter Four

Christianity: A New Dispensation

"The rise of Christianity is simply an episode of human history, not Revelation and not supernatural."[1]
                                                                    - Edmond Wilson

To learn about Christianity, we need to study the ancient philosophers and historians such as Pliny, Tacitus, Plato, Celsus and the other writers of the period. It is to these brilliant and learned men who we owe what we know of the history and beliefs of the earliest years of recorded history. What did these learned writers, teachers, philosophers and historians perceive in the new religion of Christianity? Celsus points out the "unoriginality" of these doctrines in great detail. He felt that Christianity had inherited the worst features of Judaism.

He points to:
> 1) The belief that the world was made solely for them.
> 2) The radicals monotheism and
> 3) exclusively of their beliefs.

"There is nothing new or impressive about their ethical teaching; indeed, when one compares it to other philosophies, their simple mindedness becomes apparent."[2]
                                                                    - Celsus

"Everything in Christianity, the cross, the robes and vestments, the symbols, the sacraments, the Sabbath, the festivals and holy days all preceded Christianity by thousands of years."[3]
                                                                    - Blavatsky

Heracles, the philosopher, said that some of the stories of Jesus were stolen from an earlier autobiography of Apollonius.

Philo, who died around 50 CE, lived in Palestine during the time that Christ supposedly was preaching there yet Philo never heard of him and never mentioned him in any of his "Histories".

Josephus, the Historian, born only four years after the alleged death of Christ, doesn't mention Christ's life at all and His death only in a passing remark limited to one sentence.

Suetonius, secretary to Adrian, writing in the Second Century, never mentions Jesus by name.

Adrian, writing much later, was so little impressed by the miracles and doctrines of Christ, that mistakes Christ for Serapis. The description of Christ fosters this comparison. The earliest Christians actually took the description of Serapis for their Christ. Read the following description and see if you don't agree:

Serapis was described as wearing his hair long, "formally turned back and disposed in ringlets falling down upon his breast and shoulders like that of a woman. His whole person, too, is always enveloped in drapery reaching to his feet". Serapis was further described as having a face of "grave and pensive majesty".[4] One of the titles attributed to him was "judge of the living and the dead". Sound familiar? We thought it might. It truly seems that Christ is an amalgam of many prior deities and that his followers took what they liked best from all the myths and saviors of antiquity and formed a composite that they termed Christ.

> "Christianity is shown to have originated, not in a series of unique events orchestrated by God, but by a natural process of social evolution."[5]
>
>   - A. Powell Davies

> "Christianity is grounded on certain historical events, which faith interprets, as acts of God. If these events never occurred, they were certainly not acts of God. What is most distinctive in Christian faith could not then be true."[6]
>
>   - Burrows

42

The Ten Commandments

The Ten Commandments, supposedly given directly to Moses by God were lifted with only minor changes from the Pratimoksha Sutra and other religious tracts of the Buddhists.

From the Pratimoksha Sutra we get the following:

1) Thou shalt not kill any living creature.
2) Thou shalt not steal.
3) Thou shalt not break the vow of chastity.
4) Thou shalt not lie.
5) Thou shalt not betray the secrets of others.
6) Thou shalt not wish for the death of thy enemies.
7) Thou shalt not desire the wealth of others.
8) Thou shalt not pronounce injurious or foul words.
9) Thou shalt not indulge in luxury (be lazy).
10) Thou shalt not accept gold or silver.(bribes)

This was written several centuries before Christ by the "Pagan" Buddhists, remarkable isn't it?

Hammurabi, a Babylonian King, created the earliest code of conduct c. 1728 BCE, at least four hundred years before Moses.

The Egyptian "Oath of Clearance" features six of the ten commandments, was written well before the Hebrew code and both it and the Babylonian code feature less severe commandments than the Mosaic Code.

Egyptian Oath of Clearance
(also known as The negative confession)

I have not committed fraud or evil against men.
I have not diverted justice in the judgement hall.
I have not caused a man to do more than his days work.
I have not caused a slave to be ill treated.
I have not been weak.
I have not stolen cattle.
I have not impious or impure.
I have not taken milk from the mouths of children.
I have not been wretched.....

"If a man shall put out the eye of another, then let his own eye be put out. If a man shall knock out the teeth of one higher in rank, then let his teeth be knocked out." [7]

- Hammurabi c. 1728 BCE

An unknown author writing as Moses reduced this saying to: "An eye for an eye and a tooth for a tooth." **Exodus 21:23.**

The Trinity

The papers of Theophilus c. 190 CE was the first time the concept of the trinity was used in Christian writings. The Trinity, was found in many of the early religions. The Christian statue of the Mother of God, Mary with Jesus, is a copy of the Egyptian statue of Isis and Horus. The Egyptian Trinity consisted of Osiris, Isis and Horus. In the Hindu religion we find the Trinity of Brahma, Vishnu and Siva. The concept of the Trinity was taught in the oldest Chaldean, Egyptian, and Mithric schools. The Akkadians who preceded the Babylonians, had a Trinity. The Persians had Ormazd, Mirthra and Ahriman.

The Eucharist

The Eucharist is not Christian either, as it was instituted many hundreds of years before the Last Supper. In the mysteries of Elysis celebrated in Greece, we had the elevation of a grain of wheat, in the Christian Mass, we have the elevation of a wafer of wheat (unleavened bread). The sacrifice of bread and wine was common to many nations.

"It appears that Christian theology should begin to be suspected of complete bankruptcy." [8]

- Blavatsky

"No one ignorant of the Mystery Schools and the kind of consciousness they developed can realize the blight that Christianity became. With its tortured Christ and sense of sin, it robbed us of the joy of life the earlier people knew. With its fake salvation and false God-concept, it denied us knowledge of evolution and our place and purpose in it." [9]

- Graham

The founders of Christianity took their material from Pagan mythology, rewrote it to serve their own ends, then destroyed the originals. The Christian fathers made the destruction of any and all works that showed the Pagan or Gnostic roots of their religion the first work. They went to great lengths to destroy all pagan records and so obscure their own dishonesty. By order of the church all the books of Basilides, the Gnostic were destroyed. The thirty-six volumes of Porphyry's works were also burned. Pope Gregory VII burned the entire contents of the Apollo library with a loss of thousands of ancient scrolls "lest its secular literature distract the faithful from the contemplation of heaven."[10]

The Emperor Theodosius ordered destroyed 27,000 scrolls belonging to Schools of the Mysteries because they contained the basis of the doctrines of Christianity. By offering rewards, Ptolemy gathered 270,000 ancient documents which were also burned for similar reasons. The death of learning did not end in ancient times but continued through the Middle Ages. Eighty Thousand Arabic manuscripts were ordered destroyed by Cardinal Ximenes in 1244.

> "They made dumb all pagan testimony against the unparalleled imposture then being perfected in Rome. They had almost reduced the first four centuries to silence on all matters of the most vital importance for any proper understanding of the true origins of the Christian superstition."[11]
>
> - Massey

> "The wretched world lies now under the tyranny of foolishness; things are believed by Christians of such absurdity as no one could ever aforetime induce the heathen to believe."[12]
>
> - Agobard of Lyons

It is a poor compliment, if one would call it even that, to the Supreme Being, forcing upon Him four gospels, which contain the many errors and contradictions that they do, and in which there is not a single narrative, expression, phrase, or sentence without a parallel in some older doctrine, philosophy or culture. There was some 4,000 individual writings that went into the "pool" from which the "New Testament" was derived.

When all 4,000 of the New Testament fragments are compared, over 150,000 contradictions appear. [13]

The first English version of the scriptures made by direct translation from the original Hebrew and Greek, and the first to be printed, was the work of William Tyndale. He met bitter opposition and was accused of willfully perverting the meaning of the Scriptures. His New Testaments were ordered to be burned as "untrue translations". Tyndale was finally betrayed into the hands of his enemies, and in October 1536, was publicly executed and burned at the stake. Yet Tyndale's work became the foundation of subsequent English versions, notably those of Coverdale, 1535, Thomas Matthew (probably a pseudonym for John Rogers), 1537, the Great Bible, 1539; the Geneva Bible, 1560; and the Bishops' Bible, 1568. In 1582 a translation of the New Testament, made from the Latin Vulgate by Roman Catholic scholars, was published at Rheims.

Surely, the Son of God, the chosen redeemer of mankind, in his first and only incarnation on earth, could have brought down from heaven something original.

The following popular sayings are given with their **earlier** Pagan sources.

Christian: "Blessed are the pure in heart, for they shall see god." Mat. (8:1)

Pagan: "Purity of mind alone sees god." (Manu c. 390 BCE)

Christian: "Whosoever hath, to him shall be given, but whosoever hath not, from him shall be taken away." Mat. (13:12)

Pagan: "They who give, hath things given to them, but they who withhold, have things taken from them." (Manu c. 390 BCE)

Doesn't the original saying make more sense? How can anyone take from those that have not??? Ah, but from those that have but withhold, now that makes sense at last!

Christian: "Do unto others as you would have them do unto you."

Pagan: "What I do not wish men to do to me, I also wish not to do to men." (Confucius c. 551 BCE)

Christian: "Know you that you are the temple of god, and that the spirit of god dwelleth within you?" 1 Corinthians (3:16)

Pagan: "You have within yourself something similar to god, and therefor use yourself as the temple of god." (Sextus, the Pythagorean, c. 200 CE)

Christian: "Lay not up for yourselves treasures upon earth, where moth and rust doth corrupt, and where thieves break through and steal." Mat (6:19)

Pagan: "Possess not treasures, but those things which no one can take from you" (Sextus, the Pythagorean c. 200 CE)

From an Egyptian temple inscription Circa 3100 BCE comes a fragment of a Hermetic document that states:

> "To feed the hungry, give drink to the thirsty, cloth the naked, and bury the dead ... formed the first duty of a pious man."
>
> (British Museum ,Tablet 562)

"The light of Christianity" only serves to illuminate the hypocrisy and vice that its teachings have brought into the world.

Latest Findings

The documents, which have become known as the Dead Sea Scrolls, were discovered in 1947 in caves, in the desert near Jerusalem by Bedouin nomads still living, much as their distant ancestors did. These findings throw new light on the Bible and its sagas. The discoveries and interpretations were compiled over many years by a team of experts in Biblical Research. While many lay persons might not be aware of the findings nor of their significance, most religious leaders are and most ignore the findings altogether. "Biblical Scholars were not disturbed by what they found in the Dead Sea Scrolls because they had known all along that the origin of Christianity was not what it was supposed to have been." [14]

- A. Powell Davies

The majority of devout Christians suppose that the Bible is infallible and are never told otherwise. They feel that any departure from it is a betrayal of faith. This is just not true. No one who knows the most elementary facts of the matter believes this. There are those who assume that the Greek and Hebrew texts from which our English translations of the Bible are made are infallible. No one who has studied the Bible at all could believe that. Even the most conservative of Biblical Scholars and the most conservative of churches recognize that the text has been corrupted at many points in the course of history. Faith must rest on and proceed from fact, it can never be any other way. All religions are the products of long and difficult social evolution. Christianity included.

> "If this were not already well known and universally admitted, the Dead Sea Scrolls would demonstrate it conclusively." [15]
>
> - Burrows

a) Vine/Laborers in the vineyard, borrowed from the Rites of Bacchus.

b) The Loaf from which Christ fed the multitudes; borrowed from the Rites of Ceres.

c) The Dove as Holy Ghost; borrowed from the Rites of Venus.

d) Diana's Stag became the Christian Soul panting for the Waters of Salvation.

e) Juno's Peacock became the Soul after Resurrection.

f) The Keys of Janus became St. Peter's Keys to the Church of Rome.

g) It was not until the 6th Century that the Cross was exhibited with the Body of Christ hanging upon it.

h) The Miter and Vestments of the "Head of the Church" in Rome are copies of the Tibetan Dalai Lama's.

The Basic Problem of Christianity

The basic problem with Christianity and not the only one by any means is that Christianity accents right from the very start, the good and evil problem. Christ's arrival on earth to atone for sin.

> "Evil atonement, the first people to listen to Paul were the Merchants of Corinth, and so we have the vocabulary of debt and payment. **The debt and payment explanation goes haywire when you realize there was no Garden of Eden. There was no fall of man, and there was no offense to God. So what is all this about paying a debt?"** [16]
> - Campbell

Commentary III

At this point in the book we, the authors, would like to give you, the readers, a couple of the rules of Logic by which to properly judge the truth or falseness of any written or Philosophical work.

The Foundations of Logic

Almost without predecessors on which to base his ideas and certainly by reason of his own thought processes, Aristotle created a new science, a science of right thinking. This process that Aristotle arrived at is known as Logic. The processes used today in high schools and colleges throughout the world in debates and as a foundation of scientific thought are based on Aristotle's principles. Logic is a science because like chemistry or physics, correct thinking (Logic) can be regulated by a set of rules. Aristotle's rules molded Medieval thought and was the mother of scholastic philosophy. The Essence of Logic is that all important terms be subjected to intense scrutiny and definition.

Incontestible Rules of Logic

1. The agreement of all parts of a story or narrative do not prove the truth of the whole work. The parts can all agree with one another while the entire story is still false.

2. The disagreement of any part proves the falseness of the whole because nothing can be true if any one or more parts are false.

Are you still with us so far? Good !

The story upon which Christianity is based is the story of Jesus Christ as contained in the works of Matthew, Mark, Luke and John. Agreed?

The first part of Matthew begins by giving a genealogy of Christ beginning with David, down through Joseph, and ending with Jesus. In the third chapter of Luke we also have this genealogy, but it differs somewhat. If these two accounts agreed it would still not prove the story was true but because they differ by so much, the story is conclusively false! The whole cannot be true if any of the parts are false.

If Matthew's account is true then Luke's account is false! If Luke's account is true then Matthew's account is false!

Since we have no reason to believe either one more than the other, we have to say that both are false.

Truth is uniform and must always be true! As to inspiration and Revelation, we have to assume that neither can be contradictory. God's word cannot be any less truthful or any less uniform for being inspiration or Revelation.

Either (by logic) the men called apostles are impostors or the books attributed to them were written by others, as is the case with the Old Testament. The genealogy of Jesus as given in:

Matthew (1:1)

1. David
2. Solomon
3. Roboam
4. Abia
5. Asa
6. Josaphat
7. Joram
8. Ozias
9. Joat
10. Achaz
11. Ezekis
12. Manasses
13. Amon
14. Josias
15. Jechonias
16. Salathiel
17. Zorobabel
18. Abiud
19. Eliakim
20. Azor
21. Sadoc
22. Achim
23. Eliud
24. Eleazor
25. Matthan
26. Jacob
27. Joseph
28. Christ

Luke (3:23)

1. David
2. Nathan
3. Mattatha
4. Menan
5. Melea
6. Eliakim
7. Jonan
8. Joseph
9. Juda
10. Simeon
11. Levi
12. Matthat
13. Jorim
14. Eliazer
15. Jose
16. Er
17. Elmodam
18. Cosam
19. Addi
20. Melchi
21. Neri
22. Salathiel
23. Zorobabel
24. Rhesa
25. Joanna
26. Juda
27. Joseph
28. Semei
29. Mattathias
30. Maath
31. Nagge
32. Esli
33. Naum
34. Amos
35. Mattathias
36. Joseph
37. Janna
38. Melchi
39. Levi
40. Matthat
41. Heli
42. Joseph
43. Christ

Chapter Five

The Heritage of Peter

The Garden of Eden was an ancient Goddess myth rewritten to focus on the Male God. There never was a Garden of Eden.

From the Garden, lets focus on one rock: What kind of men were Peter and his successors upon which the Church was built?

> "And I say also unto thee, thou art Peter, and upon this rock I will build my Church and the Gates of Hell shall not prevail against it."
> **(Mat. 16: 17-18)**

Unfortunately for the Popes, this passage was a forgery. It has been deliberately inserted into the scripture sometime during the 3rd century CE. It was known by historians and scholars to be a political ploy to uphold the Vatican's position against its Eastern rivals.

The designation or title "Peter" comes from the Chaldean Mysteries. The hierophant bore the title peter which meant "Interpreter."

> **"This is the "Greatest of all patristic frauds."** [1]
> - Blavatsky

Why does the author of "Isis Unveiled" make this claim? Let's look at the evidence.

The Catholic Dogma of Apostolic succession relies on Peter to have been in Rome and **Peter was never in Rome.**

Nothing in print shows that Peter was ever a real person. The scriptures concerning him were known to be forged long after the epistles of Paul were written. [2] For the first five centuries, no one ever assumed that the church of Rome had any right to rule any other congregation. Creating the fiction of Peter inheriting Christ's authority was only another tool to use in its bid for power and conquest. Pope Innocent III declared that "the Lord left to Peter the government not of the church only, but of the whole world". World domination, nothing less would do. Pope Boniface VIII declared that every man, woman and child on earth must be "subjected to the Roman Pontiff."

Was there even someone named Peter? What do you think? Was Christ a real person? We think not. **Peter, like Christ is mythology.**

The story of Peter founding the church of Rome is much like the story of the founding of Rome by Romulus and Remus. With a capacity for intellectual dishonesty, anything can be proved. The Church has opposed education and learning for the last two thousand years. Of course you can prove Peter's supremacy by quoting from the Bible but the Bible is mythology not truth and certainly not history.

And what legally have the heads of the Church of Rome gotten and passed on? What type of man does it take to become head of the Church? What type of person decides religious ideals, doctrines and ethics for all the followers of this Church?

Most of the first fifty Popes couldn't write their own names. From 891 to about 903 there were ten Popes in twelve years, and from 891 to about 1000 CE, there were forty. These divinely guided men murdered each other for the position.

Pope Boniface gained power by getting, through deceit, the eighty year old Celestine to abdicate. After receiving confirmation, Boniface had Celestine imprisoned and later, while in prison, murdered.

Sergius III murdered his two predecessors. In 708 an Italian noble had his brother appointed Pope. This was Pope Constantine II. Constantine had his eyes put out by Christopher, who served as an official of the office. Christopher also plotted against Pope Gregory, Constantine's successor. Gregory had their eyes put out as punishment.

The nephews of Leo III conspired to replace him by hiring street thugs who failed. The nephews had to complete the job themselves. This is the record of a papal biographer. Pope Leo V was deposed by another Christopher who was in turn deposed by Sergius III, mentioned previously.

Two prostitutes, Theodora and her daughter Marozia had sons by Sergius III and both sons became Popes - John XI and John XII. The first John was imprisoned. The 2nd was a murderer, who committed incest with his two sisters. It is said he died at the hand of an outraged husband.

According to what we discovered, Cardinal Francone had Pope Benedict II strangled. He then succeeded to the Papal Throne as Boniface VII. Pope Boniface VIII disposed Celestine V who was said to be a half-wit. Under the successor he was tried posthumously and found guilty of pederasty and murder. John XXII revealed that his predecessor Clement had given his nephew five million of papacy money. During this time the papal court was moved to Avignon. One successor lived at Avignon and one at Rome.

At one time in history there were three Popes: Gregory XII, Alexander V, and John XXIII. John was so corrupt that a council was called to investigate him. He was called "an oppressor of the poor, persecutor of justice, pillar of the wicked, the dregs of vice...Wholly given to sleep and carnal desires, a mirror of infamy, a profound inventor of wickedness." [3] He ascended to the throne by violence and fraud. Several popes so outraged public decency they were exiled. There were so "highly" thought of that they had their eyes and tongues cut out and were dragged through the streets tied to asses. Pope Clement VII was a holy man, nicknamed "the butcher" because of his penchant for massacre. In 1376, five thousand citizens of the town of Cesena were massacred by Papal decree. We must realize that history is full of war and conquest and as we go back, we find the church engaged in these same pursuits. The church used any and all weapons at its disposal to win for itself the position it holds today. Its weapons were bribery, forgery, and intrigue which it wielded with much relish.

Church history is entwined with that of the kings and Bishops who were its advocates in the field against rivals, and, just as warring kings fought, so the church fought also with elaborate hoaxes that are accepted as truth by many today.

Early Popes were often only names taken from Pagan literature, of Roman gods inserted into scripture to show a false chronology back to Peter. Even Catholic scholars will today admit that the stories of Peter were fictitious.

Several were so highly regarded that after their deaths, their bodies were dug up and thrown into the Tiber River. This only takes us up to the Borgias.

Rodrigo Borgias bribed fifteen cardinals to get the papacy as Alexander VI. He was described as having private habits of the utmost obscenity. Cesare Borgia murdered his brother John, his sister's husband, and two cardinals to become Pope. According to the Papal Historian of the time, he indulged in nightly revels with naked courtesans.

Paul III appointed two of this teenage grandchildren as Cardinals. Paul IV made his nephew a Cardinal. None of this is common knowledge, but it is there if you look hard enough.

Denial of Christ

The denial by Peter of Christ has ritualistic overtones and was copied from earlier Pagan traditions as well. Remember that nothing in the Bible is new or unique. It all comes from earlier Pagan mythology. Even if the source seems somewhat obscure or difficult to find, searching has proven a sure recourse, its all there in pagan mythology. This same denial occurs in the religion of Canaan where the dying god is denied by one of his priests.

Chapter Six

The Spirit of Christianity

"I have a son, and no one but God knows how I love him, but I would see those beautiful eyes dug out of his head tonight, rather than see him grow to manhood and go down to the grave without Christ and without hope!" [1]

- Moody (The Revivalist)

"Resist not evil, but whosoever shall smite thee on thy right cheek, turn to him the other also."

Matthew (5:39)

"Judge not lest ye be judged."

Matthew (7:1)

"Give to him who asketh of thee, and from him that would borrow of thee, turn not away."

Matthew (5:42)

During the Renaissance, artists celebrated the beauty of the naked female body on canvas while in dungeons and in the streets women were being tortured and burned by the thousands by the tribunals of the "Holy" Inquisition. In Medieval and Renaissance Europe, the Catholic Church not only endorsed slavery but introduced it into places where it had never existed before. In the tenth century, Bishop Ratherius of Varona stated the following: "God has mercifully destined those for slavery for whom He saw that freedom was not fitting." [2] Christianity's labor record is equally atrocious. The church has always viewed hard, unrelieved labor and class inequality as fitting punishment for "original" sin.

The world record for mass killings is held by Christians. Millions of human beings, in the last 2,000 years have been tortured and killed, in a number of hideous ways all in the name of Christ.

Is this the true basis for Christian belief? "Let us do evil that good may come."

Romans 3:7-8

"It is an act of virtue to deceive and lie, when by such means the interests of the church might be promoted."

- Ecclesiastical History,
vol 1, pgs 381-382

In magazines and newspapers you will find no end to stories of child abuse, torture and murder to "free" someone, most often children, from Satan's clutches, as examples, we offer the following:

1) In 1976, a Christian fundamentalist sect was involved in the beating death of a three year old boy, whose parents were members of the sect they beat the "Devil" out of him, and life also. Is this what Christ asks of his followers?

2) In Philadelphia, in 1979, a 3 month old baby was thrown out of a 2nd story window by his aunt, who revealed to police that the Lord told her to because the child was sinful.

3) Another story from 1979 comes from Hampton, Va., where a mother cut off the right hand of her 5 year old daughter, her seven year old daughter's left hand and her own because she had been reading the Bible story about John the Baptist's beheading. (We fail to see the similarity of a "beheading" and cutting off your hand, but maybe we're too logical.)

4) In New York, in 1980, a 21 month old boy was scalded by his mother while three brothers watched because he had to be "exorcised." The mother told police that she had to get the Devil out of her baby.

5) Also in 1980, in Austin, Texas, a 21 year old man was sleeping in his truck with his head against the window one night when his friend drove up and killed him thinking he was the devil because, his friend told police he had been discussing the Devil with his girlfriend earlier in the evening.

6) In 1983, in California, a 2½ year old child was held against a floor heater until the Devil left her and she died.

7) In 1984, in Bangor, Maine, a man killed his girlfriend's 4 year old daughter by burning her in an electric oven, claiming she was Lucifer.

> "And whosoever shall offend one of these little ones which believeth in me, it were better for him that a millstone were hanged about his neck and that he were drowned in the depths of the sea."
>
> **Matthew 18:6**

The quote says "offend", how much worse must it be to injure or kill "one of these little ones."

8) In Utah, in a town called American Fork, in 1984, two brothers forced their way into their sister-in-law's home while her husband was at work and killed her, and her daughter in the crib. God had told them that it was "His" will that these people should be removed.

9) In a Wisconsin town, in 1985, a man claiming to be "Elijah" the prophet shot and killed a priest, and two parishioners for allowing a girl to read scripture during mass. He claimed he was doing "God's will."

It's very hard to determine exactly how many people are killed around the world for their beliefs or disbelief. Only the most tragic stories come to light. Many less tragic, stories of "less human interest" never get printed at all because they lack the selling power of the more obscene murders but the point is: **historically it has never been "Satanic cults" (where and if they exist at all) that have endangered the life or limb of anyone on any scale approaching that of the Christians.**

The world has been endangered, and still is today by weak, simple minded, gibbering, Bible packing "righteous," fundamentalist, "moral" people "working for God" or "enlisted in Christ's army, doing the Lord's work". Today's modern army recruits on college campuses to ensure that its leaders are at least trainable for positions of leadership. It's too bad that there isn't any "fitness" test required for "The Lord's Army" as there is in others.

Any religion that attempts to "explain" human suffering, injustice, hunger poverty, or homelessness as manifestations of God's will cannot be a valid religion. It is an attempt by the power hungry elite to maintain that control and power. We, as a people deserve better.

Any religion that supports a "dominance-submission" social structure is seeking to control others.

To reduce people to something "sinful" is to make them exploitable. We have to deny anyone the right to do this.

"The Christian church has set up a system of religion, very contradictory to the character of the person whose name it bears."[3]
- Thomas Paine

The Biblical God and his religion are based on a violently antisexual morality never before seen in any other civilization or time period anywhere on earth. In the Christian religion there is one overriding commandment: Punish life for being what it is.

Chapter Seven

The Origin Of Evil

It is a common axiom that the gods of one religion become the devils of the next.

1. Set / Satan was the god of the ancient Hittites.[1]

2. Beelzebub was an oracular god, similar to the Grecian Apollo.

3. Asmodeus is Persian, originally a Devi (little god).

4. Diabolos was a name derived from Atabul-os, "the wind of the desert."

5. Plutarch remarks that the name Typhon was given to anything violent, unruly, or disorderly. A concept not an individual.[2]

6. Three and a half centuries before Christ, Plato expressed an opinion of evil that said "There is in matter, a blind force, which resists the will of the Great Artificer". This "blind force", under Christian influence became the devil, combined with the accumulating gods of conquered peoples.

7. It is not the devil under any name, that causes evil anyway. The Bible tells us where evil comes from in **Isaiah (45:7)**. It is God himself that causes evil.

8. Lucifer, originally god of the morning star, announced the birth of the sun each morning. The name means "light bringer". The Canaanites called him Shaher. The Jewish morning service called Shaharit still commemorates him. Shaher is said to have had a twin brother, who was called Shalem, the evening star. It was Shalem's responsibility to announce the death of the sun each day.

    "How art thou fallen from heaven, O Lucifer, son of the morning...
    For thou hast said in thine heart, I will ascend to heaven, I will
    exalt my throne above the stars of God; I will sit also upon the
    mount of the congregation, in the sides of the north; I will ascend
    above the heights of the clouds; I will be like the most High."
    Isaiah 14:12-14

Is Isaiah saying anything original here? Of course not! EVERYTHING in the Bible is plagiarized from other sources -- everything! What Isaiah is supposed to have said is copied from a 7th century dirge for the fallen Morning Star and was originally written centuries before as follows:

> "How hast thou fallen from heaven, Helel's son Shaher! Thou didst say in thy heart, I will ascend to heaven, above the circumpolar stars I will raise my throne, and I will dwell on the Mount of council in the back of the north; I will mount on the back of a cloud, I will be like unto Elyon." [3]

Actually it appears to be a common goal of rulers in those days to aspire to ascend into heaven and become one with the god and rule with him in heaven. An inscription found on an Egyptian Pharaoh's tomb stated that he "standeth upon the north of heaven with Ra, he becometh lord of the universe like unto the king of the gods."

If we lose devils, we would lose the Savior also. For from whom or what would the Savior be needed to save us? Then there would be no more Redeemer, for from whom or what would the Redeemer redeem us? Then there would be no more Christianity. Christianity needs Satan to survive. If the concept of Satan were tampered with, the very foundation of Christianity would crumble.

So what's the difference between demons and devils, aren't they really the same thing?

Demons

According to St. Thomas of Aquinas, bad weather, storms and natural catastrophes are brought about by demons. "It is a dogma of faith that demons produce wind, storms, and rain of fire from heaven." [4] Pope Eugene IV issued a bull against human "agents of Satan" who control weather demons.

The church had several theories about the origin of demons, we will present two of them here. The two are contradictory in nature.

One theory said that demons were rebellious angels cast into Hell with Lucifer by God. This happened before the creation of Adam and Eve and so was intended to lend support to that story. A second theory that is incompatible with the first states that demons were created when "the sons of God saw the daughters of men, that they were fair" and came down from heaven and mated with them as stated in Genesis 6:4. Some "authorities" familiar with Pagans' animal masks and with animal headed deities such as worshiped in Egyptian, held the opinion that demons were an animal like race of spirits created separately by God. These spirits often inhabited the physical bodies of animals such as Black goats, cats and dogs. There is a story about St. Ambrose leaving his church and

60

exorcising the frogs in the marsh outside to get them to stop croaking during mass. History does not record his success or lack of it. During 1474, a rooster committed the most unnatural of acts by laying an egg. The unfortunate rooster was exorcised and after this failed to rid him of the devil he was burned at the stake.

A Dominican Friar, Raymond of Tarrega, a town in Spain, said that demons were useful for punishing the sinners in Hell and that they therefor were doing God's will. It was Friar Raymond's opinion that people could adore demons "so long as we adore, not their evil, but their existence, which was given them by God." He stated further "It is not desirable to sacrifice to demons, but to do so is no more serious than adoring an image of Christ or the saints."[5] Later, his opinion was overturned and the Inquisition burned his book.

Devils

The words "devil" and "divinity" come from the same root, the Persian Devi, which meant "little god". It became divell in old English and has been traced to the Roman "divi" which meant a generic "gods". One mans god was his enemies devil, the same with warring factions and countries. Even early Christians sometimes said that the "devils" worshiped in pagan temples were known to heal the sick and infirm.

It was not uncommon, in the early days of the church, to hear mention of seven devils, one assigned to each of the seven "deadly" sins. The list follows:

1. Pride: Lucifer
2. Avarice: Mammon
3. Lechery: Asmodeus
4. Anger: Satan
5. Gluttony: Beelzebub
6. Envy: Leviathan
7. Sloth: Belphegor

Most of the mythology connected with the devil or devils attribute certain almost god-like qualities to him (most devils were the gods of conquered people so this isn't really surprising). Attributes like god-like intelligence, sexuality, and cunning. One of the inquisitors, a certain Jean Bodin, wrote "It is certain that the devils have a profound knowledge of all things. No theologian can interpret Holy Scriptures better than they can; no lawyer has more detailed knowledge of testaments, contracts and actions; no physician or philosopher can better understand the composition of the human body, and the virtues of the heavens, the stars, birds and fishes...."[6]

With thinking like this, it isn't hard to see why theologians have such a problem explaining why God allows the devil so much freedom of action or why He seems powerless to stop him.

Chapter Eight

Women: A Viewpoint

"By Law, public sentiment and religion, from the time of Moses down to the present day, woman has never been thought of as other than a piece of property to be disposed of at the will and pleasure of men." [1]
- Susan B. Anthony

"Men are holy, who know not women."
Samuel 21:4

"Every woman should be overwhelmed with shame at the very thought that she is a woman." [2]
- St. Clement

"Among all savage beasts, none is found so harmful as a women."[3]
- St. John Chrysostom

"To be fully developed as a human being is to be born a male." [4]
- Thomas Aquinas

"If the world could be rid of women, we should not be without God."[5]
- Cato of Utica
(Catholic Theologian)

"When Eve was created, Satan rejoiced." [6]
- Mohammed

In his "Vindication of Married Life", Martin Luther stated that men must continue to maintain their power over women, "since man is higher and better than she." [7]

The suppression, even in our supposedly enlightened age, of women's rights stems from the much earlier suppression of women's rites by the newly established male oriented religion. Ah, but it doesn't stop there, there is more! Please read on.

"Therefore as the Church is subject unto Christ, so let wives be unto their own husbands in everything."

Ephasians 5: (22 - 24)

"Blessed art thou O Lord our God, King of the Universe, who has not made me a woman." [8]

- Hebrew Prayer

The Ecumenical Council that met at Macon in or about 900 CE decided by only a **one vote margin** that women even had souls.

"Let the woman learn in silence with all subjection. But I suffer not a woman to teach, nor to usurp authority over the man, but to be in silence."

Timothy 2: (11 -14)

"The head of every man is Christ; and the head of every woman is the man; and the head of Christ is God. For a man indeed should not cover his head for as much as he is the image and glory of God, but the woman is the glory of the man. For the man is not of the woman; but the woman is of the man. Neither was man created for the woman but for the man."

I Corinthians 11: (3 - 9)

"Likewise ye wives, be in subjection to your own husbands, for after this manner in the old time, the holy women also, who trusted in God, adorned themselves, being in subjection to their husbands."

I Peter 3: 1

St. Augustine claimed that man, but not woman, was made in God's image and woman therefore is not complete without man, while he is complete alone.

"If a woman grows weary and at last dies from child bearing, it matters not, for she is there to do it." [9]

- Martin Luther

"Man enjoys the great advantage of having a God endorse the code he writes; and since man exercises a sovereign authority over women, it is especially fortunate that his authority has been vested in him by the Supreme Being. For the Jews, Mohammedans, and Christians among others, man is master by divine right, the fear of God will therefore repress any impulse toward revolt in the down trodden female." Taken from "The Second Sex" by Simone De Beauvoir.

An Episcopal Bishop was quoted in 1971 saying:
 "The sexuality of Christ is no accident nor is his masculinity incidental." [10]

If you are a woman, reading this, can you really afford to be Christian?

In 1486 it was officially declared that "no one does more harm to the Catholic faith than midwives." [11] Why was this? Because women were meant to suffer as God's punishment to Eve (who never existed in the first place). Women who attended the poor during childbirth were frequently made social outcasts, charged with doing the devil's work, tortured and burned. There exists an account of a woman in Scotland who was burned alive for bathing some neighborhood children during an epidemic. Healthcare and healing were discouraged by the church whose official stance was that life is supposed to be full of misery and suffering because it was God's will and punishment for the sin of being born.

And if that isn't enough... During the "Middle Ages" in Catholic dominated Europe, it was a crime for a woman to miscarry. Even if a woman miscarried as the result of an accident or a beating by her husband, she could be put to death for her sin against God. What kind of God would demand such a thing? A good, just and loving father? Or a misogynic priesthood straining for dominance and power?

All miscarriages were seen by the "holy fathers" as deliberate attempts at abortion and were punishable by death. Thus says the celibate priesthood of this "loving" God. The warring factions of matter versus spirit, or sexual versus religious are inventions of the present patriarchal period forced on humanity only in recent times. Neither had any place among earlier religions or races and neither is natural or true.

Chapter Nine

Before the Coming of "Enlightened" Christianity

"At the time of Iamblichus (373 CE) the Priests of Egypt owned forty two books that they attributed to Hermes. Of these, thirty-six contained the history of all human knowledge; the last six treated of anatomy, of pathology, of affections of the eye, instruments of surgery and of medicines." One of these written on the inner bark of a papyrus "consisted of a single sheet 3/10 of a meter wide, more than 20 meters long, forming one roll divided into 110 pages, all carefully numbered."[1]

- Durant

It has been found that the calendars of the Aztecs are so accurate, that no error has been discovered in several verifications, while the reformed Julian calendar was off by nearly eleven days.

In the Abbot Egyptological collection in New York City are kept numerous artifacts of the skills of the ancient Civilizations among these are exhibits of:

        The Art of Lace Making
        Specimens of Artificial Hair
        Gold Ornaments
        Hair Growth Invigorators
        Hair Dyes
        Pain Killers
        Flea Powders

Other achievements of the 'uncivilized' Pagans:

In Babylon was a series of Chaldean astronomical observations, going back 1903 years that Callistenes sent to Aristotle.

A record of eclipses going back 747 years possessed by Ptolemy, the Egyptian King and astronomer.

The Babylonians had fixed the length of the tropical year within 23 seconds.

An estimate of the sidereal year off by barely 2 minutes in Babylon.

A Babylonian record of the procession of the equinoxes.

The Babylonians also had:

- A knowledge of the cause of eclipses and predictions of them.

- An estimate of the solar cycle of more than 6,585 days that was within 19.5 minutes.

- A correct view of the structure of the Solar System and the order and placement of the planets.

They had constructed sun dials, astrolabes, and other instruments.

It was the 'superstitious' Pagans that gave us math, science, law, architecture, and the basis for the U.S. Constitution and the Bill of Rights.

"Whoa there, son" you say, "the Bill of Rights and the United States Constitution were written by our Christian forefathers who came over on the Mayflower etc. weren't they?" Actually, the U.S. Constitution and Bill of Rights were composed by Thomas Jefferson, John Q. Adams, Thomas Paine and James Madison, none of whom were Christian. All four were Deists and based the Constitution and Bill of Rights on the Great Law of Peace of the Longhouse people: the Iroquois Nation. The founding fathers were so impressed by this Law, by its sanity and wisdom that they incorporated much of it's spirit and some of its organizational details into the U.S. Constitution. To this degree the Constitution is a true living expression or our original American Pagan heritage.

In fact, evidence shows that some of the most advanced societies of the ancient world - both technologically as well as culturally - were Pagan, Goddess-oriented (Matrifocal). Crete was one of these and was the major cultural and trading center of its day.

The people of Crete had:
Indoor Baths
Hot & Cold Running Water
Ceramic Pipes

All in 1700 BCE, a feat not achieved by Christian Europe until well after 1700 CE, 3400 years later.

The graceful and artistic Etruscans were also matrifocal as were the early Egyptians.

The 'educated' Christian Priesthood at this period in time still believed that the Earth was flat. A good two hundred years after Magellan proved that the earth was round, Catholic educators were still insisting that it was flat. An argument of the day was that the earth had to be flat because if it were round "in the day of judgement men on the other side of a globe could not see the Lord descending through the air." Concerning earth's motion St. Augustine had this to say: "It is impossible there should be inhabitants on the opposite side of the earth, since no such race is recorded by Scripture among the descendants of Adam." [2] Yet as early as the sixth century Pythagoras had taught that the earth was round and circled the sun. As early as the third century Eratosthenes had a measurement of the circumference of the earth and during the second century Hipparchus had invented latitude, longitude and discovered the procession of the equinoxes. The "brilliant" catholic educators threw out learning en-masse.

These same 'brilliant' minds maintained that the Earth was the center of the Universe and the Sun revolved around the Earth. The Clergy made it a heresy to believe anything else.

> **"The opinion of the Earth's motion is of all heresies the most abominable, the most pernicious, the most scandalous; the immobility of the Earth is thrice sacred."** [3]
>
> - Father Inchofer

In 1893, an encyclical of Pope Leo XIII declared that no scholar could interpret the Bible contrary to established church beliefs. This encyclical further stated that the church is never wrong. Pope Pius X bitterly opposed scholarly study of the Bible as late as the twentieth century.

Christianity has always contradicted known truths throughout history and enthusiastically and bitterly opposed learning and science for the last several thousand years.

Christians said that one of the most diabolic symptoms of the upcoming end of the world was the spread of knowledge.

By the end of the fifth century, the rulers of Christianity had succeeded in forcibly stopping the study of philosophy, mathematics, medicine and geography preferring the mass of lay persons be dumb rather than risk anyone learning the truth.

Pope Gregory denounced education as "folly and wickedness." [4]

Chapter Ten

The "Good Book" Up Close

In 1965, the Catholic Church's Dogmatic Constitution declared all books of the Bible are "accurate, true, and without error." Keeping that in mind please examine and explain the following:

Blood For Blood

For your lifeblood I will surely require a reckoning; of every beast I will require it and of man; of every man's brother I will require the life of man. Whoever sheds the blood of man, by man shall his blood be shed.

Genesis 9:5,6

Not Blood For Blood

Then the Lord said to him, "Not so! If any one slays Cain, vengeance shall be taken on him sevenfold."

Genesis 4:15

A Command

You must not make a carved image for yourself, nor the likeness of anything in the heavens above, or on the earth below, or in the waters under the earth.

Exodus 20:4

A Command Contradicted

And you shall make two cherubim of gold... The cherubim shall spread out their wings above, overshadowing the mercy seat with their wings...

Exodus 25:18, 20

Noah said, "Cursed be Canaan; a slave of slaves shall he be to his brothers."
Genesis 9:25

You may bequeath them to your sons after you, to inherit as a possession for ever; you may make slaves of them.
Leviticus 25:46

I will sell your sons and your daughters into the hand of the sons of Judah and they will see them to the Sabens, to a nation far off; for the Lord has spoken."
Joel 3:8

Slavery Forbidden

"Is not this the fast that I choose; to loose the bonds of wickedness, to undo the thongs of the yoke, to let the oppressed go free, and to break every yoke?"
Isaiah 58:6

"Whoever steals a man, whether he sells him or is found in possession of him, shall be put to death."
Exodus 21:16

Neither be called masters, for you have one master, the Christ.
Matthew 23:10

Laziness Commended

And why are you anxious about clothing? Consider the lilies of the field, how they grow; they neither toil nor spin...
Matthew 6:28, 31, 34

Sell your possessions, and give alms; provide yourselves with purses that do not grow old, with a treasure in the heavens that does not fail...
Luke 12:33

Laziness Condemned

If any one does not provide for his relatives, and especially for his own family, he has disowned the faith and is worse than an unbeliever.
1 Timothy 5:8

A good man leaves an inheritance to his children's children, but the sinner's wealth is laid up for the righteous.

Proverbs 13:22

Circumcision Commanded

He that is eight days old among you shall be circumcised; every male throughout your generations.

Genesis 17:10

Circumcision Not Commanded

Now I, Paul, say to you that if you receive circumcision, Christ will be of no advantage to you.

Galatians 5:2

Keep The Sabbath

Remember the Sabbath day, to keep it holy.

Exodus 20:8

Do Not Keep The Sabbath

Bring no more vain offerings; incense is an abomination to me. New moon and Sabbath and the calling of assemblies -- I cannot endure iniquity and solemn assembly.

Isaiah 1:13

One man esteems one day as better than another, while another man esteems all days alike.

Romans 14:5

Therefore let no one pass judgment on you in questions of food and drink or with regard to a festival or a new moon or a Sabbath.

Colossians 2:16

Why The Sabbath Was Instituted

For in six days the Lord made heaven and earth, the sea, and all that is in them, and rested the seventh day; therefore the Lord blessed the Sabbath day and hallowed it.

Exodus 20:11

You shall remember that you were a servant in the land of Egypt, and the Lord your God brought you out thence with a mighty hand and an outstretched arm; therefore the Lord your God commanded you to keep the Sabbath day.

Deuteronomy 5:15

Work Not On The Sabbath

Six days shall work be done, but the seventh day is a Sabbath of solemn rest, holy to the Lord; whoever does any work on the Sabbath day shall be put to death.

Exodus 31:15

While the people of Israel were in the wilderness, they found a man gathering sticks on the Sabbath day... And all the congregation brought him outside the camp, and stoned him to death with stones, as the Lord commanded Moses.

Numbers 15:32, 36

Work On The Sabbath

And this was why the Jews persecuted Jesus, because he did this on the Sabbath.

John 5:16

At that time Jesus went through the grainfields on the Sabbath; his disciples were hungry, and they began to pluck heads of grain and to eat. But when the Pharisees say it, they said to him, "Look, your disciples are doing what is not lawful to do on the Sabbath." He said to them, "Have you not read what David did, when he was hungry, and those who were with him... Or have you not read in the law how on the Sabbath the priests in the temple profane the Sabbath, and are guiltless?

Matthew 12:1, 2, 3, 5

Become Angry

Be angry but do not sin; do not let the sun go down on your anger...

Ephesians 4:26

Do Not Become Angry

Be not quick to anger, for anger lodges in the bosom of fools.

Ecclesiastes 7:9

Make no friendship with a man given to anger, nor go with a wrathful man...
Proverbs 22:24

For the anger of man does not work the righteousness of God.
James 1:20

How You Must Do

Let your light so shine before men, that they may see your good works and give glory to your Father who is in heaven.
Matthew 5:16

How You Must Not Do

Beware of practicing your piety before men in order to be seen by them; for then you will have no reward from your Father who is in heaven.
Matthew 6:1

Judge Not

Judge not, that you be not judged. For with the judgment you pronounce you will be judged, and the measure you give will be the measure you get.
Matthew 7:1, 2

Judging Permitted

Do you not know that the saints will judge the world? And if the world is to be judged by you, are you incompetent to try trivial cases? Do you not know that we are to judge angels? How much more, matters pertaining to this life! If then you have such cases, why do you lay them before those who are least esteemed by the church?
1 Corinthians 6:2, 3, 4

For what have I to do with judging outsiders? Is it not those inside the church whom you are to judge?
1 Corinthians 5:12

Resisting Evil

But I say to you, Do not resist one who is evil. But if any one strikes you on the right cheek, turn to him the other also.
Matthew 5:39

But they said, "Not during the feast, least there be a tumult among the people... You know that after two days the Passover is coming, and the Son of man will be delivered up to be crucified.

Matthew 26:5, 2

Physical Resistance Commended

He said to them, "But now, let him who has a purse take it, and likewise a bag. And let him who has no sword sell his mantle and buy one.

Luke 22:36

And making a whip of cords, he drove them all, with the sheep and oxen, out of the temple; and he poured out the coins of the money-changers and overturned their tables.

John 2:15

Christ Said "Be Not Afraid."

"I tell you, my friends, do not fear those who kill the body, and after that have no more that they can do."

Luke 12:4

Christ Was Afraid

And this Jesus went about in Galilee; he would not go about in Judea, because the Jews sought to kill him.

John 7:1

Public Prayer Is Permitted

Then Solomon stood before the altar of the Lord in the presence of all the assembly of Israel, and spread forth his hands toward heaven... Now as Solomon finished offering all this prayer and supplication to the Lord, he arose from before the altar of the Lord, where he had knelt with hands outstretched toward heaven; and he stood, and blessed all the assembly of Israel with a loud voice... And the Lord said to him, "I have heard your prayer and your supplication, which you have made before me; I have consecrated this house which you have built, and put my name there for ever; my heart will be there for all time.

1 Kings 8:22, 54 & 9:3

Public Prayer Is Not Permitted

"And when you pray, you must not be like the hypocrites; for they love to stand and pray in the synagogues and at the street corners, that they may be seen by men. Truly, I say to you, they have received their reward. But when you pray, go into your room and shut the door and pray to your Father who is in secret; and your Father who sees in secret will reward you.

Matthew 6:5, 6

Permitted To Wear Long Hair

"For lo, you shall conceive and bear a son. No razor shall come upon his head, for the boy shall be a Nazirite to God from birth; and he shall begin to deliver Israel from the hand of the Philistines."

Judges 13:5

"All the days of his vow of separation no razor shall come upon his head; until the time is completed for which he separates himself to the Lord, he shall be holy; he shall let the locks of hair of his head grow long."

Numbers 6:5

Not Permitted To Wear Long Hair

Does not nature itself teach you that for a man to wear long hair is degrading to him.

1 Corinthians 11:14

Baptizing Permitted

Go therefore and make disciples of all nations, baptizing them in the name of the Father and of the Son and of the Holy Spirit...

Matthew 28:19

Baptizing Not Permitted

For Christ did not send me to baptize but to preach the gospel, and not with eloquent wisdom, lest the cross of Christ be emptied of its power.

1 Corinthians 1:17, 14

All Animals Can Be Used For Food

Every moving thing that lives shall be food for you; and as I gave you the green plants, I give you everything.

Genesis 9:3

Eat whatever is sold in the meat market without raising any question on the ground of conscience.

1 Corinthians 10:25

I know and am persuaded in the Lord Jesus that nothing is unclean in itself; but it is unclean for any one who thinks it is unclean.

Romans 14:14

All Animals Can Not Be Used For Food

Yet of those that chew the cud or have the hoof cloven you shall not eat these: The camel, the hare, and the rock badger, because they chew the cud but do not part the hoof, are unclean for you. And the swine, because its parts the hoof but does not chew the cud, is unclean for you. Their flesh you shall not eat, and their carcasses you shall not touch.

Deuteronomy 14:7, 8

Oaths Permitted

When a man vows a vow to the Lord, or swears an oath to bind himself by a pledge, he shall not break his word; he shall do according to all that proceeds out of his mouth.

Numbers 30:2

Now, therefore swear to me here by God that you will not deal falsely with me or with my offspring or with my posterity, but as I have dealt loyally with you, you will deal with me and with the land where you have sojourned. And Abraham said, "I will swear." herefore that place was called Beer-sheba; because there both of them swore an oath.

Genesis 21:23, 24, 31

The God of Abraham and the God of Nahor, the God of their father, judge between us." So Jacob swore by the Fear of his father Isaac.

Genesis 31:53

For when God made promise to Abraham, because he could swear by no greater, he sware by himself.

Hebrews 6:13

Oaths Not Permitted

But I say to you, Do not swear at all, either by heaven, for it is the throne of God...

Matthew 5:34

Marriage Not Permitted With Sister

"Cursed be he who lies with his sister, whether the daughter of his father or the daughter of his mother.' And all the people shall say, 'Amen.'

Deuteronomy 27:22

If a man takes his sister, a daughter of his father or a daughter of his mother and sees her nakedness, and she sees his nakedness, it is a shameful thing and they shall be cut off in the sight of the children of their people; he has uncovered his sister's nakedness, he shall bear his iniquity.

Leviticus 20:17

Marriage Permitted With Sister

Abraham said, "I did it because I thought, there is no fear of God at all in this place, and they will kill me because of my wife... Besides she is indeed my sister, the daughter of my father but not the daughter of my mother; and she became my wife.

Genesis 20:11, 12

Permitted To Marry Brother's Widow

If brothers dwell together, and one of them dies, and has no son, the wife of the dead shall not be married outside the family to a stranger; her husband's brother shall go in to her, and take her as his wife, and perform the duty of a husband's brother to her.

Deuteronomy 25:5

Not Permitted To Marry Brother's Widow

If a man takes his brother's wife, it is impurity; he has uncovered his brother's nakedness; they shall be childless.

Leviticus 20:21

Hatred Is Permitted

If any one comes to me and does not hate his own father and mother and wife and children and brothers and sisters, yes, and even his own life, he cannot be my disciple.

Luke 14:26

Hatred Is Not Permitted

Husbands, love your wives, as Christ loved the church and gave himself up for her. For no man ever hates his own flesh, but nourishes and cherishes it, as Christ does the church.

Ephesians 5:25, 29

Any one who hates his brother is a murderer, and you know that no murderer has eternal life abiding in him.

1 John 3:15

Anti-Prohibitionist

Give strong drink to him who is perishing. Let them drink and forget their property, and remember their misery no more.

Proverbs 31:6, 7

No longer drink only water, but use a little wine for the sake of your stomach and your frequent ailments.

1 Timothy 5:23

And wine to gladden the heart of man, oil to make his face shine, and bread to strengthen man's heart.

Psalms 104:15

Not Anti-Prohibitionist

Wine is a mocker, strong drink a brawler;

Proverbs 20:1

Do not look at wine when it is red, when it sparkles in the cup and goes down smoothly.

Proverbs 23:31, 32

Marriage Advisable

Then the Lord God said, "It is not good that the man should be alone; I will make him a helper fit for him."

Genesis 2:18

And God blessed them, and God said to them, "Be fruitful and multiply, and fill the earth and subdue it; and have dominion over the fish of the sea and over the birds of the air and over every living thing that moves upon the earth.

Genesis 1:28

And said, For this reason a man shall leave his father and mother and be joined to his wife, and the two shall become one flesh?

Matthew 19:5

Let marriage be held in honor among all, and let the marriage bed be undefiled; for God will judge the immoral and adulterous.

Hebrews 13:4

Marriage Not Advisable

Now concerning the matters about which you wrote. It is well for a man not to touch a woman.

1 Corinthians 7:1

Now concerning the things where-of ye write unto me: It is good for a man not to touch a woman. I would that all men were even as myself. But man hath his proper gift of God, one after this matter, and another after that. I say therefore to the unmarried and widows, It is good for them if they abide even as I.

1 Corinthians 7:1, 7, 8

Divorce Allowed

When a man takes a wife and marries her, if then she finds no favor in his eyes because he has found some indecency in her, and he writes her a bill of divorce and puts it in her hand and sends her out of his house, and she departs out of his house...

Deuteronomy 24:1

"When you go forth to war against your enemies, and the Lord your God gives them into your hands, and you take them captive, and see among the captives a beautiful woman, and you have desire for her and would take her for yourself as wife. Then, if you have no delight in her, you shall let her go where she will; but you shall not sell her for money, you shall not treat her as a slave, since you have humiliated her.

Deuteronomy 21:10, 11, 14

Divorce Restricted

But I say to you that every one who divorces his wife, except on the ground of unchastity, makes her an adulteress; and whoever marries a divorced woman commits adultery.

Matthew 5:32

Do Not Commit Adultery

You shall not commit adultery.

Exodus 20:14

Let marriage be held in honor among all, and let the marriage bed be undefiled; for God will judge the immoral and adulterous.

Hebrews 13:4

Yes, You May Commit Adultery

But all the woman children, that have not known a man by lying with him, keep alive for yourselves.

Numbers 31:18

When the Lord first spoke through Hosea, the Lord said to Hosea, "Go, take to yourself a wife of harlotry and have children of harlotry, for the land commits great harlotry by forsaking the Lord." Say to your brother, "My people," and to your sister, "She has obtained pity." Plead with your mother, plead - for she is not my wife, and I am not her husband - that she put away her harlotry from her face, and her adultery from between her breasts; lest I strip her naked and make her as in the day she was born, and make her like a wilderness, and set her like a parched land, and slay her with thirst.

Hosea 1:2 & 2:1, 2, 3

A Plain Statement

Let every person be subject to the governing authorities. For there is no authority except from God, and those that exist have been instituted by God... Therefore he who resists the authorities resists what God has appointed, and those who resist will incur judgment... For rulers are not a terror to good conduct, but to bad. Would you have no fear of him who is in authority? Then do what is good, and you will receive his approval. For the same reason you also pay taxes, for the authorities are ministers of God, attending to this very thing.

Romans 13:1, 2, 3, 6

The scribes and the Pharisees sit on Moses' seat; so practice and observe whatever they tell you, but not what they do; for they preach, but do not practice.

Matthew 23:2, 3

Be subject for the Lord's sake to every human institution, whether it be to the emperor as supreme, or to governors as sent by him to punish those who do wrong and to praise those who do right.

1 Peter 2:13, 14

The Discrepancy

But the midwives feared God, and did not do as the king of Egypt commanded them, but let the male children live.

Exodus 1:17, 20

Shadrach, Meshach, and Abednego answered the king, "O Nebuchadnezzar, we have no need to answer you in this matter. But if not, be it known to you, O king, that we will not serve your gods or worship the golden image which you have set up."

Daniel 3:16, 18

Therefore King Darius singed the document and interdict... All the presidents of the kingdom, the prefects and the satraps, the counselors and the governors are agreed that the king should establish an ordinance and enforce an interdict, that whoever makes petition to any god or man for thirty days, except to you, O king, shall be cast into the den of lions. When Daniel knew that the document had been signed, he went to his house where he had windows in his upper chamber open toward Jerusalem; and he got down upon his knees three times a day and prayed and gave thanks before his God, as he had done previously.

Daniel 6:9, 7, 10

The kings of the earth set themselves in array, and the rulers were gathered together, against the Lord and against his Anointed for truly in this city there were gathered together against thy holy servant Jesus, whom thou didst anoint, both Herod and Pontius Pilate, with the Gentiles and the peoples of Israel.

Acts 4:26, 27

And in his teaching he said, "Beware of the scribes, who like to go about in long robes, and to have salutations in the market places and the best seats in the synagogues and the places of honor at feasts, who devour windows; houses and for a pretense make long prayers. They will receive the greater condemnation."

Mark 12:38, 39, 40

And Herod with his soldiers treated him with contempt and mocked him; then, arraying him in gorgeous apparel, he sent him back to Pilate, So Pilate gave sentence that their demand should be granted. And when they came to the place which is called The Skull, there they crucified him, and the criminals, one on the right and one on the left... And the people stood by, watching; but the rulers scoffed at him, saying, "He saved others; let him save himself, if he is the Christ of God, his Chosen One!"

Luke 23:11, 24, 33, 35

They Went By Sevens

Then the Lord said to Noah, "Go into the ark, you and all your household, for I have seen that you are righteous before me in this generation. Take with you seven pairs of all clean animals, the male and his mate; and a pair of the animals that are not clean, the male and his mate. And Noah did all that the Lord had commanded him.

Genesis 7:1, 2, 5

They Went By Twos

Of clean animals, and of animals that are not clean, and of birds and of everything that creeps on the ground, two and two, male and female, went into the ark with Noah, as God had commanded Noah.

Genesis 7:8, 9

Seed Time And Harvest Shall Not Cease

While the earth remains, seedtime and harvest, cold and heat, summer and winter, day and night, shall not cease.

Genesis 8:22

Seed Time And Harvest Did Cease For Seven Years

And the seven years of famine began to come, as Joseph had said. There was famine in all lands; but in all the land of Egypt there was bread... So when the famine had spread over all the land, Joseph opened all the storehouses, and sold to the Egyptians, for the famine was severe in the land of Egypt.

Genesis 41:54, 56

For the famine has been in the land these two years; and there are yet five years in which there will be neither plowing nor harvest.

Genesis 45:6

God Did It

And the Lord said to Moses, "When you go back to Egypt, see that you do before pharaoh all the miracles which I have put in your power; but I will harden his heart, so that he will not let the people go.

Exodus 4:21

But the Lord hardened the heart of Pharaoh, and he did not listen to them; as the Lord had spoken to Moses.

Exodus 9:12

The Pharaoh Did It

But when Pharaoh saw that there was a respite, he hardened his heart, and would not listen to them; as the Lord had said.

Exodus 8:15

All The Cattle And Horses Died

Behold, the hand of the Lord will fall with a very severe plague upon your cattle which are in the field, the horses, the asses, the camels, the herds, and the flocks... And on the morrow the Lord did this thing; all the cattle of the Egyptians died, but of the cattle of the people of Israel not one died.

Exodus 9:3, 6

All The Cattle And Horses Did Not Die

The Egyptians pursued them, all Pharaoh's horses and chariots and his horsemen and his army, and overtook them encamped at the sea.

Exodus 14:9

Women Keep Quiet

To the woman he said, "I will greatly multiply your pain in childbearing; in pain you shall bring forth children, yet your desire shall be for your husband, and he shall rule over you."

Genesis 3:16

I permit no woman to teach or to have authority over men; she is to keep silent.

1 Timothy 2:12

The women should keep silence in the churches. For they are not permitted to speak, but should be subordinate, as even the law says.

1 Corinthians 14:34

As Sarah obeyed Abraham, calling him lord. And you are now her children if you do right and let nothing terrify you.

1 Peter 3:6

Women's Rights

Now Deb'orah, a prophetess, the wife of Lap'pidoth, was judging Israel at that time... And Deb'orah said to Barak, "Up! For this is the day in which the Lord has given Sis'era into your hand. Does not the Lord go out before you?" So Barak went down from Mount Tabor with ten thousand men following him. And the Lord routed Sis'era and all his chariots and all his army before Barak at the edge of the sword; and Sis'era alighted from his chariot and fled away on foot.

Judges 4:4, 14, 15

The peasantry ceased in Israel, they ceased until you arose, Deb'orah, arose as a mother in Israel.

Judges 5:7

Yea, and on my menservants and my maidservants in those days I will pour out my Spirit; and they shall prophesy.

Acts 2:18

And he had four unmarried daughters, who prophesied.

Acts 21:9

Serve Your Master

Slaves, obey in everything those who are your earthly masters, not with eyeservice, as men-pleasers, but in singleness of heart, fearing the Lord... Whatever your task, work heartily, as serving the Lord and not men.

Colossians 3:22, 23

Servants, be submissive to your masters with all respect, not only to the kind and gentle but also to the overbearing.

1 Peter 2:18

86

Serve Only God

Then Jesus said to him, "Begone, Satan! for it is written, You shall worship the Lord your God and him only shall you serve.

Matthew 4:10

You were bought with a price; do not become slaves of men.

1 Corinthians 7:23

Neither be called masters, for you have one master, the Christ.

Matthew 23:10

An Unpardonable Sin

But whoever blasphemes against the Holy Spirit never has forgiveness, but is guilty of an eternal sin.

Mark 3:29

No Unpardonable Sin

And by him every one that believes is freed from everything from which you could not be freed by the law of Moses.

Acts 13:39

Moses Feared

He answered, "Who made you a prince and a judge over us? Do you mean to kill me as you killed the Egyptian?" Then Moses was afraid, and thought, "Surely the thing is known." When Pharaoh heard of it, he sought to kill Moses. But Moses fled from Pharaoh, and stayed in the land of Mid'ian; he sat down by a well... In the course of those many days the king of Egypt died. And the people of Israel groaned under their bondage, and cried out for help, and their cry under bondage came up to God... And the Lord said to Moses in Mid'ian, "Go back to Egypt; for all the men who were seeking your life and dead.

Exodus 2:14, 15, 23 & 4:19

Moses Did Not Fear

By faith he left Egypt, not being afraid of the anger of the king; for he endured as seeing him who is invisible.

Hebrews 11:27

Nevertheless those that died by the plague were twenty-four thousand.

Numbers 25:9

23,000 Died

We must not indulge in immortality as some of them did, and twenty-three thousand fell in a single day.

1 Corinthians 10:8

This Is Eli'jah

And if you are willing to accept it, he is Eli'jah who is to come.

Matthew 11:14

This Is Not Eli'jah

And they asked him, "What then! Are you Eli'jah?" He said, "I am not." "Are you the prophet?" And he answered, "No."

John 1:21

Father Of Joseph Was Jacob

She will bear a son, and you shall call his name Jesus, for he will save his people from their sins.

Matthew 1:16

Father Of Joseph Was Heli

Jesus, when he began his ministry, was about thirty years of age, being the son (as was supposed) of Joseph, the son of Heli.

Luke 3:23

Arphaxad Was Father Of Shelah

When Arphaxad had lived thirty-five years, he became the father of Shelah.

Genesis 11:12

Arphaxad Was Father Of Cainan

The son of Serug, the son of Re'u, the son of Shelah. The son of Ca-i'nan, the son of Arpha'xad, the son of Shem, the son of Noah, the son of Lamech.
Luke 3:35, 36

Christ Delivered First Sermon On Mount

Seeing the crowds, he went up on the mountain, and when he sat down his disciples came to him.
Matthew 5:1, 2

Christ Delivered First Sermon On Plain

And he came down with them and stood on a level place, with a great crowd of his disciples and a great multitude of people from all Judea and Jerusalem and the seacoast of Tyre and Sidon, who came to hear him and to be healed of their diseases...
Luke 6:17, 20

Was It John In Prison?

Now after John was arrested, Jesus came into Galilee, preaching the gospel of God.
Mark 1:14

It Was Not John In Prison?

The next day Jesus decided to go to Galilee. And he found Philip and said to him, "Follow me."
John 1:43

After this Jesus and his disciples went into the land of Judea; there he remained with them and baptized. John also was baptizing at Ae'non near Salim, because there was much water there; and people came and were baptized. For John had not yet been put in prison.
John 3:22, 23, 24

Woman Of Canaan Sought Jesus

And behold, a Canaanite women from that region came out and cried, "Have mercy on me, O Lord, Son of David; my daughter is severely possessed by a demon.
Matthew 15:22

Now the woman was a Greek, A Syrophoenician by birth. And she begged him to cast the demon out of her daughter.

Mark 7:26

14 Generations From Abraham To David

So all the generations from Abraham to David were fourteen generations, and from David to the deportation to Babylon fourteen generations, and from the deportation to Babylon to the Christ fourteen generations.

Matthew 1:17

13 Generations From Abraham To David

The book of the genealogy of Jesus Christ, the son of David, the son of Abraham... and Jesse the father of David the king. And David was the father of Solomon by the wife of Uriah.

Matthew 1:2, 6

14 Generations From Babylonian Capture To Christ

So all the generations from Abraham to David were fourteen generations, and from David to the deportation to Babylon fourteen generations, and from the deportation to Babylon to the Christ fourteen generations.

Matthew 1:17

13 Generations From Babylonian Capture To Christ

And after the deportation to Babylon; Jechoniah was the father of Shealtiel, and Shealtiel the father of Zerubbabel... and Jacob the father of Joseph the husband of Mary, of whom Jesus was born, who is called Christ.

Matthew 1:12, 16

Jesus Taken Into Egypt

And he rose and took the child and his mother by night, and departed to Egypt, and remained there until the death of Herod. This was to fulfil what the Lord had spoken by the prophet, "Out of Egypt have I called my son." But when Herod died, behold, an angel of the Lord appeared in a dream to Joseph in Egypt... and he went and dwelt in a city called Nazareth, that what was spoken by the prophets might be fulfilled, "He shall be called a Nazarene."

Matthew 2:14, 15, 19, 23

Jesus Not Taken Into Egypt

And when the time came for their purification according to the law of Moses, they brought him up to Jerusalem to present him to the Lord... And when they had performed everything according to the law of the Lord, they returned into Galilee, to their own city, Nazareth.

Luke 2:22, 39

Christ Tempted In The Wilderness

The Spirit immediately drove him out into the wilderness. And he was in the wilderness forty days, tempted by Satan; and he was with the wild beasts; and the angels ministered to him.

Mark 1:12, 13

Christ Not Tempted In The Wilderness

After this he went down to Caper'na-um, with his mother and his brothers and his disciples; and there they stayed for a few days.

John 2:12

Two Blind Men

And behold, two blind men sitting by the roadside, when they heard that Jesus was passing by, cried out.

Matthew 20:30

One Blind Man

As he drew near to Jericho, a blind man was sitting by the roadside begging.

Luke 18:35, 38

Crucified At Third Hour

And it was the third hour, when they crucified him.

Mark 15:25

Now it was the day of Preparation of the Passover; it was about the sixth hour. He said to the Jews, "Behold your King!" They cried out, "Away with him, away with him, crucify him!" Pilate said to them, "Shall I crucify your King!" The chief priests answered, "We have no king but Caesar."

John 19:14, 15

Two Thieves Reviled Christ

Then two robbers were crucified with him, one on the right and one on the left. And the robbers who were crucified with him also reviled him in the same way.

Matthew 27:38, 44

Let the Christ, the King of Israel, come down now from the cross, that we may see and believe." Those who were crucified with him also reviled him.

Mark 15:32

One Thief Reviled Christ

One of the criminals who were hanged railed at him, saying, "Are you not the Christ? Save yourself and us!" But the other rebuked him, saying "Do you not fear God, since you are under the same sentence of condemnation?"

Luke 23:39, 40

Satan Taketh Possession Of Judas While At Supper

Jesus answered, "It is he to whom I shall give this morsel when I have dipped it." So when he had dipped the morsel, he gave it to Judas, the son of Simon Iscariot. Then after the morsel, Satan entered into him. Jesus said to him, "What you are going to do, do quickly.

John 13:26, 27

Satan Taketh Possession Of Judas Before Supper

Then Satan entered into Judas called Iscariot, who was of the number of the twelve; he went away and conferred with the chief priests and officers how he might betray him to them. Then came the day of unleavened Bread, on which the passover lamb had to be sacrificed.

Luke 22:3, 4, 7

Judas Hung Himself

And throwing down the pieces of silver in the temple, he departed; and he went and hanged himself.

Matthew 27:5

Judas Did Not Hang Himself

Now this man bought a field with the reward of his wickedness; and falling headlong he burst open in the middle and all his bowels gushed out.

Acts 1:18

Two Angels Seen

But Mary stood weeping outside the tomb, and as she wept she stooped to look into the tomb; and she saw tow angels in white, sitting where the body of Jesus had lain, one at the head and one at the feet.

John 20:11, 12

One Angel Seen

And entering the tomb, they saw a young man sitting on the right side, dressed in a white robe; and they were amazed.

Mark 16:5

Three Days & Three Nights In The Grave

For as Jonah was three days and three nights in the belly of the whale, so will the Son of man be three days and three nights in the heart of the earth.

Matthew 12:40

Two Days & Two Nights In The Grave

And it was the third hour, when they crucified him. And when evening had come, since it was the day of Preparation, that is, the day before the Sabbath. And Pilate wondered if he were already dead; and summoning the centurion, he asked him whether he was already dead. And when he learned from the centurion that he was dead, he granted the body to Joseph. And he bought a linen shroud, and taking him down, wrapped him in the linen shroud, and laid him in a tomb which had been hewn out of rock; and he rolled a stone against the door of the tomb. Now when he rose early on the first day of the week, he appeared first to Mary Magdalene, from whom he had cast out seven demons.

Mark 15:25, 42, 44, 45, 46 & 16:9

But you shall receive power when the Holy Spirit has come upon you; and you shall be my witnesses in Jerusalem and in all Judea and Samaria and to the end of the earth... for John baptized with water, but before many days you shall be baptized with the Holy Spirit.

Acts 1:8, 5

When the day of Pentecost has come, they were all together in one place. And they were all filled with the Holy Spirit and began to speak in other tongues, as the Spirit gave the utterance.

Acts 2:1, 4

Holy Ghost Given Before Pentecost

And when he had said this, he breathed on them, and said to them, "Receive the Holy Spirit.

John 20:22

Go Into Galilee

Then Jesus said to them, "Do not be afraid; go and tell my brethren to go to Galilee, and there they will see me."

Matthew 28:10

Tarry At Jerusalem

And behold, I send the promise of my Father upon you; but stay in the city, until you are clothed with power from on high.

Luke 24:49

Judas Purchased A Field

Now this man bought a field with the reward of his wickedness; and falling headlong he burst open in the middle and all his bowels gushed out.

Acts 1:18

Chief Priest Purchased A Field

But the chief priests, taking the pieces of silver, said, "It is not lawful to put them into the treasury, since they are blood money."... So they took counsel, and bought with them the potter's field, to bury strangers in.

Matthew 27:6, 7

Only One Woman Came To The Sepulcher

Now on the first day of the week, Mary Magdalene came to the tomb early, while it was still dark, and saw that the stone had ben taken away from the tomb.

John 20:1

Two Women Came To The Sepulcher

Now after the Sabbath, toward the dawn of the first day of the week, Mary Magdalene and the other Mary went to see the sepulchre.

Matthew 28:1

Three Women Came To The Sepulcher

And when the Sabbath was past, Mary Magdalene, and Mary the mother of James, and Salome, bought spices, so that they might go and anoint him.

Mark 16:1

More Than Three Women Came To The Sepulcher

Now it was Mary Magdalene and Joanna and Mary the mother of James and the other women with them who told this to the apostles.

Luke 24:10

At Sunrise They Visited The Sepulcher

And very early on the first day of the week they went to the tomb when the sun had risen.

Mark 16:2

Sometime Before Sunrise They Visited The Sepulcher

Now on the first day of the week, Mary Magdalene came to the tomb early, while it was still dark, and saw that the stone had ben taken away from the tomb.

John 20:1

And they rose that same hour and returned to Jerusalem; and they found the eleven gathered together and those who were with them. As They were saying this, Jesus himself stood among them. And he said to them, "Why are you troubled, and why do questionings rise in your hearts.

Luke 24:33, 36, 37

On the evening of that day, the first day of the week, the doors being shut where the disciples were, for fear of the Jews, Jesus came and stood among them and said to them, "Peace be with you." Now Thomas, one of the twelve, called the Twin, was not with them when Jesus came.

John 20:19, 24

Jesus Makes Appearance To Eleven Disciples On A Mountain In Galilee

Now the eleven disciples went to Galilee, to the mountain to which Jesus had directed them. And when they saw him they worshiped him; but some doubted.

Matthew 28:16, 17

Christ's Ascent Was From Mt. Olivet

And when he had said this, as they were looking on, he was lifted up, and a cloud took him out of their sight.

Acts 1:9, 12

Christ's Ascent Was From Bethany

Then he led them out as far as Bethany, and lifted up his hands he blessed them. While he blessed them, he parted from them, and was carried up into heaven.

Luke 24:50, 51

Heard The Strange Voice

The men who were traveling with him stood speechless, hearing the voice but seeing no one.

Acts 9:7

Did Not Hear The Strange Voice

And when we had all fallen to the ground, I heard a voice saying to me in the Hebrew language, 'Saul, Saul, why do you persecute me? It hurts you to kick against the goads.'

Acts 26:14

Abraham Started For Canaan

And Abram took Sarai his wife, and Lot his brother's son, and all their possessions which they had gathered, and the persons that they had gotten in Haran: and they set forth to go to the land of Canaan.

Genesis 12:5

Abraham Did Not Know Where He Was Going

By faith Abraham obeyed when he was called to go out to a place which he was to receive as an inheritance; and he went out, not knowing where he was to go.

Hebrews 11:8

Ahaziah Was The Youngest Son

And the inhabitants of Jerusalem made Ahaziah his youngest son king in his stead.

2 Chronicles 22:1

Ahaziah Was Not The Youngest Son

And the Lord stirred up against Jehoram the anger of the Philistines and of the Arabs who are near the Ethiopians... and they came up against Judah, and invaded it, and carried away all the possessions they found that belonged to the king's house, and also his sons and his wives, so that no son was left to him except Jehoahaz, his youngest son.

2 Chronicles 21:16, 17

In The Twelfth Year

In the twelfth year of Joram the son of Ahab, king of Israel, Ahaziah the son of Jehoram, king of Judah, began to reign.

2 Kings 8:25

In the eleventh year of Joram the son of Ahab, Ahaziah began to reign over Judah.

2 Kings 9:29

Did The Lord Tempt David To Number Israel

Again the anger of the Lord was kindled against Israel, and he incited David against them, saying, "Go, number Israel and Judah."

2 Samuel 24:1

Did Satan Tempt David To Number Israel

Satan stood up against Israel, and incited David to number Israel.

1 Chronicles 21:1

Abraham Had Two Sons

For it is written that Abraham had two sons, one by a slave and one by a free woman.

Galatians 4:22

Abraham Had One Son

By faith Abraham, when he was tested, offered up Isaac, and he who had received the promises was ready to offer up his only son.

Hebrews 11:17

Keturah Was His Wife

Abraham took another wife, whose name was Keturah.

Genesis 25:1

Keturah was His Concubine

The sons of Keturah, Abraham's concubine.

1 Chronicles 1:32

God Promised

The Lord said to Abram, after Lot had separated from him, "Lift up your eyes, and look from the place where you are, northward and southward and eastward and westward; for all the land which you see I will give to you and to your descendants for ever. And I will give to you, and to your descendants after you, the land of your sojournings, all the land of Canaan, for an everlasting possession; and I will be their God."

Genesis 13:14, 15 & 17:8

God's Promises Not Fulfilled

Yet he gave him no inheritance in it, not even a foot's length, but promised to give it to him in possession and to his posterity after him, though he had no child.

Acts 7:5

By faith he sojourned in the land of promise, as in a foreign land, living in tents with Isaac and Jacob, heirs with him of the same promise.

Hebrews 11:9, 13

Israel Had 800, 000 Fighting Men, Judah 500,000

And Joab gave the sum of the numbering of the people to the king: in Israel there were eight hundred thousand valiant men who drew the sword, and the men of Judah were five hundred thousand.

2 Samuel 24:9

Israel Had 1,100,000 Fighting Men, Judah 470,000

And Joab gave the sum of the numbering of the people to David. In all Israel there were one million one hundred thousand men who drew the sword, and in Judah four hundred and seventy thousand who drew the sword.

1 Chronicles 21:5

David Sinned

But David's heart smote him after he had numbered the people. And David said to the Lord, "I have sinned greatly in what I have done. But now, O Lord, I pray thee, take away the iniquity of thy servant; for I have done very foolishly."

2 Samuel 24:10

Because David did what was right in the eyes of the Lord, and did not turn aside from anything that he commanded him all the days of his life, except in the matter of Uriah the Hittite.

1 Kings 15:5

Seven Years Of Famine

So Gad (the Lord's prophet) came to David and told him, and said to him, "Shall three years of famine come to you in your land? Or will you flee three months before your foes while they pursue you? Or shall there be three days' pestilence in your land? Now consider, and decide what answer I shall return to him who sent me."

2 Samuel 24:13

Three Years Of Famine

So Gad came to David and said to him, "Thus says the Lord, "Take which you will;... either three years of famine; or three months of devastation by your foes, while the sword of your enemies overtakes you; or else three days of the sword of the Lord, pestilence upon the land, and the angel of the Lord destroying throughout all the territory of Israel.

1 Chronicles 21:11, 12

He Captured 700 Horsemen

And David took from him a thousand chariots, and seven hundred horsemen, and twenty thousand foot soldiers; and David hamstrung all the chariot horses, but left enough for a hundred chariots.

2 Samuel 8:4

He Captured 7,000 Horsemen

And David took from him a thousand chariots, seven thousand horsemen, and twenty thousand foot soldiers; and David hamstrung all the chariot horses, but left enough for a hundred chariots.

1 Chronicles 18:4

50 Shekels Of Silver

But the king said to Araunah, "No, but I will buy it of you for a price; I will not offer burnt offerings to the Lord my God which cost me nothing." So David bought the threshing floor and the oxen for fifty shekels of silver.

2 Samuel 24:24

600 Shekels Of Gold

So David paid Ornan six hundred shekels of gold by weight for the site.

1 Chronicles 21:25

Christ And God Equal

I and the Father are one.

John 10:30

Who, though he was in the form of God, did not count equality with God a thing to be grasped.

Philippians 2:6

Christ Not God's Equal

You heard me say to you, 'I go away, and I will come to you.' If you loved me, you would have rejoiced, because I go to the Father; for the Father is greater than I.

John 14:28

But of that day and hour no one knows, not even the angels of heaven nor the Son, but the Father only.

Matthew 24:36

Jesus Omnipotent

And Jesus came and said to them, "All authority in heaven and on earth has been given to me.

Matthew 28:18

The Father loves the Son, and has given all things into his hand.

John 3:35

And he could do no mighty work there, except that he laid his hands upon a few sick people and healed them.

Mark 6:5

Peace

And suddenly there was with the angel a multitude of the heavenly host praising God and saying, "Glory to God in the highest, and on earth peace among men with whom he is pleased!"

Luke 2:13, 14

No Peace

"Do not think that I have come to bring peace on earth; I have not come to bring peace, but a sword."

Matthew 10:34

No Testimony From Men

There is another who bears witness to me, and I know that the testimony which he bears to me is true... Not that the testimony which I receive is from man; but I say this that you may be saved.

John 5:33, 34

Testimony From Men

And you also are witnesses, because you have been with me form the beginning.

John 15:27

My Record Is True

I bear witness to myself, and the Father who sent me bears witness to me... Jesus answered, "Even if I do bear witness to myself, my testimony is true, for I know whence I have come and whither I am going, but you do not know whence I come or whither I am going.

John 8:18, 14

My Record Is Not True

If I bear witness to myself, my testimony is not true.

John 5:31

Christ Died For His Friends

Greater love has no man that this, that a man lay down his life for his friends.

John 15:13

Christ Died For The Faithful

I am the good shepherd. The good shepherd lays down his life for the sheep.

John 10:11

Christ Died For His Enemies

For if while we were enemies we were reconciled to God by the death of his Son, much more, now that we are reconciled, shall we be saved by his life.

Romans 5:10

Lawful For Jews To Kill Christ

The Jews answered him, "We have a law, and by that law he ought to die, because he has made himself the Son of God."

John 19:7

Not Lawful For Jews To Kill Christ

Pilate said to them, "Take him yourselves and judge him by your own law." The Jews said to him "It is not lawful for us to put any man to death."

John 18:31

Permitted To Punish Children

You shall not bow down to them or serve them; for I the Lord your God am a jealous God, visiting the iniquity of the fathers upon the children to the third and the fourth generation of those who hate me.

Exodus 20:5

The soul that sins shall die. The son shall not suffer for the iniquity of the father, nor the father suffer for the iniquity of the son; the righteousness of the righteous shall be upon himself, and the wickedness of the wicked shall be upon himself.

Ezekiel 18:20

Man Justified By Faith Only

For no human being will be justified in his sight by works of the law, since through the law comes knowledge of sin.

Romans 3:20

Yet who knows that a man is not justified by works of the law but through faith in Jesus Christ, even we have believed in Christ Jesus, in order to be justified by faith in Christ, and not by works of the law, because by works of the law shall no one be justified.

Galatians 2:16

Are you so foolish? Having begun with the Spirit, are you now ending with the flesh?... Now it is evident that no man is justified before God by the law; for "He who through faith is righteous shall live"... but the law does not rest on faith, for "He who does them shall live by them."

Galatians 3:3, 11, 12

For if Abraham was justified by works, he has something to boast about but not before God.

Romans 4:2

Man Not Justified By Faith Only

Was not Abraham our father justified by works, when he offered his son Isaac upon the altar?... You see that a man is justified by works and not by faith alone.

James 2:21, 24

For it is not the hearers of the law who are righteous before God, but the doers of the law who will be justified.

Romans 2:13

Can Not Fall From Grace

And I give them eternal life, and they shall never perish, and no one shall snatch them out of my hand.

John 10:28

For I am sure that neither death, nor life, nor angels, nor principalities, nor things present, nor things to come, nor powers, nor height, nor depth, nor anything else in all creation, will be able to separate us from the love of God in Christ Jesus our Lord.

Romans 8:38, 39

Can Fall From Grace

But when a righteous man turns away from his righteousness and commits iniquity and does the same abominable things that the wicked man does, shall he live? None of the righteous deeds which he has done shall be remembered; for the treachery of which he is guilty and the sin he has committed, he shall die.

Ezekiel 18:24

For it is impossible to restore again to repentance those who have once been enlightened, who have tasted the heavenly gift, and have become partakers of the Holy Spirit, and have tasted the goodness of the word of God and the powers of the age to come, if they then commit apostasy, since they crucify the Son of God on their own account and hold him up to contempt.

Hebrews 6:4, 5, 6

For if, after they have escaped the defilements of the world through the knowledge of our Lord and Savior Jesus Christ, they are again entangled in them and overpowered, the last state has become worse for them than the first. For it would have been better for them never to have known the way of righteousness than after knowing it to turn back from the holy commandment delivered to them.

2 Peter 2:20, 21

God Satisfied

And God saw everything that he had made, and behold, it was very good. And there was evening and there was morning, a sixth day.

Genesis 1:31

And the Lord was sorry that he had made man on the earth, and it grieved him to his heart.

Genesis 6:6

God Chooses A Temple

Then the Lord appeared to Solomon in the night and said to him: "I have heard your prayer, and have chosen this place for myself as a house of sacrifice... For now I have chosen and consecrated this house that my name may be there for ever; my eyes and my heart will be there for all time.

2 Chronicles 7:12, 16

God Does Not Chose A Temple

Yet the Most High does not dwell in houses made with hands; as the prophet says...

Acts 7:48

God Resides In Light

Who alone has immortality and dwells in unapproachable light, whom no man has ever seen or can see. To him be honor and eternal dominion.

1 Timothy 6:16

God Resides In Darkness

Then Solomon said, "The Lord has set the sun in the heavens, but has said that he would dwell in thick darkness.

1 Kings 8:12

He made darkness his covering around him, his canopy thick clouds dark with water.

Psalms 18:11

Clouds and thick darkness are round about him; righteousness and justice are the foundation of his throne.

Psalms 97:2

God Speaks

Then I will take away my hand until I have passed by.

Exodus 33:23

Thus the Lord used to speak to Moses face to face, as a man speaks to his friend. When Moses turned again into the camp, his servant Joshua the son of Nun, a young man, did not depart from the tent.

Exodus 33:11

But the Lord God called to the man and said to him, "Where are you?" And he said, "I heard the sound of thee in the garden, and I was afraid, because I was naked; and I hid myself."

Genesis 3:9, 10

So Jacob called the name of the place Peniel, saying, "For I have seen God face to face, and yet my life is preserved."

Genesis 32:30

In the year that King Uzziah died I saw the Lord sitting upon a throne, high and lifted up; and his train filled the temple.

Isaiah 6:1

Then Moses and Aaron, Nadab, and Abihu, and seventy of the elders of Israel went up, and they saw the God of Israel; and there was under his feet as it were a pavement of sapphire stone, like the very heaven for clearness. And he did not lay his hand on the chief men of the people of Israel; they beheld God, and ate and drank.

Exodus 24:9, 10, 11

God Cannot Be Seen Or Heard

No one has ever seen God; the only Son, who is in the bosom of the Father, he has made him known.

John 1:18

And the Father who sent me has himself borne witness to me. His voice you have never heard, his form you have never seen.

John 5:37

"But," he said, "you cannot see my face; for man shall not see me and live."

Exodus 33:20

Who alone has immortality and dwells in unapproachable light, whom no man has ever seen or can see. To him be honor and eternal dominion.

1 Timothy 6:16

God Comprehends The Nature Of Man

And they prayed and said "Lord, who knowest the hearts of all men, show which one of these two thou hast chosen.

Acts 1:24

Thou knowest when I sit down and when I rise up; thou discernest my thoughts from afar.

Psalms 139:2, 3

God Does Not Comprehend The Nature Of Man But Tries

You shall not listen to the words of that prophet or to that dreamer of dreams; for the lord your God is testing you, to know whether you love the Lord your God with all your heart and with all your soul.

Deuteronomy 13:3

And you shall remember all the way which the Lord your God has led you these forty years in the wilderness, that he might humble you, testing you to know what was in your heart, whether you would keep his commandments, or not.

Deuteronomy 8:2

He said, "Do not lay your hand on the lad or do anything to him; for now I know that you fear God, seeing you have not withheld your son, your only son, from me.

Genesis 22:12

God Omnipotent

"Behold, I am the Lord, the God of all flesh; is anything too hard for me?"

Jeremiah 32:27

But Jesus looked at them and said to them, "With men this is impossible, but with God all things are possible."

Matthew 19:26

108

God Is Not Omnipotent

And the Lord was with Judah, and he took possession of the hill country, but he could not drive out the inhabitants of the plain, because they had chariots of iron.

Judges 1:19

God Does Not Change

Every good endowment and every perfect gift is from above, coming down from the Father of lights with whom there is no variation or shadow due to change.

James 1:17

"For I the Lord do not change; therefore you, O sons of Jacob, are not consumed.

Malachi 3:6

I the Lord have spoken; it shall come to pass, I will do it; I will not go back, I will not spare, I will not repent; according to your ways and your doings I will judge you, says the Lord God."

Ezekiel 24:14

God is not man, that he should lie, or a son of man, that he should repent. Has he said, and will he not do it? Or has he spoken, and will he not fulfil it?

Numbers 23:19

God Is Changeable

And the Lord was sorry that he had made man on the earth, and it grieved him to his heart.

Genesis 6:6

When God saw what they did, how they turned from their evil way, God repented of the evil which he had said he would do to them; and he did not do it.

Jonah 3:10

Therefore the Lord the God of Israel declares: I promised that your house and the house of your father should go in and out before me for ever; but now the Lord declares: 'Far be it from me; for those who honor me I will honor, and those who despise me shall be lightly esteemed. Behold, the days are coming, when I will cut off your strength and the strength of your father's house, so that there will not be an old man in your house.

1 Samuel 2:30, 31

In those days Hezekiah became sick and was at the point of death, and Isaiah the prophet the son of Amoz came to him, and said to him, "Thus says the Lord, 'Set your house in order; for you shall die, you shall not recover.'"... And before Isaiah had gone out of the middle court, the word of the Lord came to him: "Turn back, and say to Hezekiah the prince of my people, Thus says the Lord, the God of David your father: I have heard your prayer, I have seen your tears; behold, I will heal you; on the third day you shall go up to the house of the Lord. And I will add fifteen years to your life. I will deliver you and this city out of the hand of the king of Assyria, and I will defend this city for my own sake and for my servant David's sake.

2 Kings 20:1, 4, 5, 6

The Lord said to Moses, "Depart, go up hence, you and the people whom you have brought up out of the land of Egypt, to the land of which I swore to Abraham, Isaac, and Jacob, saying, 'To your descendants I will give it.'... Go up to a land flowing with milk and honey; but I will not go up among you lest I consume you in the way, for you are a stiff-necked people"... And the Lord said to Moses, "This very thing that you have spoken I will do; for you have found favor in my sight, and I know you by name."... And he said, "My presence will go with you, and I will give you rest."

Exodus 33:1, 3, 17, 14

God Is Weary

"It is a sign for ever between me and the people of Israel that in six days the Lord made heaven and earth, and on the seventh day he rested, and was refreshed."

Exodus 31:17

You have rejected me, says the Lord, you keep going backward; so I have stretched out my hand against you and destroyed you; I am weary of relenting.

Jeremiah 15:6

God Is Never Weary

Have you not known? Have you not heard? The Lord is the everlasting God, the Creator of the ends of the earth. He does not faint or grow weary, his understanding is unsearchable.

Isaiah 40:28

God Is Omnipresent

Whither shall I go from thy Spirit? Or whither shall I flee from thy presence?

Psalms 139:7, 10

110

There is no gloom or deep darkness where evildoers may hid themselves... For his eyes are upon the ways of a man, and he sees all his steps.

Job 34:22, 21

God Is Not Omnipresent

And the Lord came down to see the city and the tower, which the sons of men had built.

Genesis 11:5

Then the Lord said, "Because the outcry against Sodom and Gomorrah is great and their sin is grave, I will go down to see whether they have don altogether according to the outcry, which has come to me; and if not, I will know."

Genesis 18:20, 21

And they heard the sound of the Lord God walking in the garden in the cool of the day, and the man and his wife hid themselves from the presence of the Lord God among the trees of the garden.

Genesis 3:8

The Lord Is Just

To show that the Lord is upright; he is my rock, and there is no unrighteousness in him.

Psalms 92:15

"Far be it from thee to do such a thing, to slay the righteous with the wicked, so that the righteous fare as the wicked! Far be that from thee! Shall not the Judge of all the earth do right?"

Genesis 18:25

"The Rock, his work is perfect; for all his ways are justice. A God of faithfulness and without iniquity, just and right is he.

Deuteronomy 32:4

For God shows no partiality.

Romans 2:11

"Yet you say, 'The way of the Lord is not just.' Hear now, O house of Israel: Is my way not just? Is it not your ways that are not just?"

Ezekiel 18:25

The Lord Is Not Just

He said, "Cursed be Canaan; a slave of slaves shall he be to his brothers."

Genesis 9:25

"You shall not bow down to them or serve them; for I the Lord your God am a jealous God, visiting the iniquity of the fathers upon the children to the third and the fourth generation of those who hate me."

Exodus 20:5

Though they were not yet born and had done nothing either good or bad, in order that God's purpose of election might continue, not because of works but because of his call. She was told, "The elder will serve the younger." As it is written, "Jacob I loved, but Esau I hated."

Romans 9:11, 12, 13

For to him who has will more be given, and he will have abundance; but from him who has not, even what he has will be taken away.

Matthew 13:12

The Lord Causes Evil

Is it not from the mouth of the Most High that good and evil come?

Lamentations 3:38

Now, therefore, say to the men of Judah and the inhabitants of Jerusalem: "Thus says the Lord, Behold, I am shaping evil against you and devising a plan against you. Return, every one from his evil way, and amend your ways and your doings."

Jeremiah 18:11

Is a trumpet blown in a city, and the people are not afraid? Does evil befall a city, unless the Lord has done it?

Amos 3:6

Moreover I gave them statutes that were not good and ordinances by which they could not have life...

Ezekiel 20:25

The Lord Does Not Cause Evil

For God is not a God of confusion but of peace.

1 Corinthians 14:33

112

"The Rock, his work is perfect; for all his ways are justice. A God of faithfulness and without iniquity, just and right is he.

Deuteronomy 32:4

Blessed is the man who endures trial, for when he has stood the test he will receive the crown of life which God has promised to those who love him.

James 1:12

God Freely Assists Those Who Ask

If any of you lacks wisdom, let him ask God, who gives to all men generously and without reproaching, and it will be given him.

James 1:5

For every one who asks receives, and he who seeks finds, and to him who knocks it will be opened.

Luke 11:10

God Cruelly Withholds Assistance From Those Who Ask

He has blinded their eyes and hardened their heart, lest they should see with their eyes and perceive with their heart, and turn for me to heal them.

John 12:40

For it was the Lord's doing to harden their hearts that they should come against Israel in battle, in order that they should be utterly destroyed, and should receive no mercy but be exterminated, as the Lord commanded Moses.

Joshua 11:20

O Lord, why doest thou make us err from thy ways and harden our heart, so that we fear thee not? Return for the sake of thy servants, the tribes of thy heritage.

Isaiah 63:17

Those Who Seek God Will Find Him

For every one who asks receives, and he who seeks finds, and to him who knocks it will be opened.

Matthew 7:8

I love those who love me, and those who seek me diligently find me.

Proverbs 8:17

113

Then they will call upon me, but I will not answer; they will seek me diligently but will not find me.

Proverbs 1:28

The Lord Is A Man Of War

The Lord is a man of war; the Lord is his name.

Exodus 15:3

For I am the Lord your God, who stirs up the sea so that its waves roar - the Lord of hosts is his name.

Isaiah 51:15

The Lord Is Peaceful

The God of peace be with you all. Amen.

Romans 15:33

For God is not a God of confusion but of peace.

1 Corinthians 14:33

God Delights In Burnt Offerings

And every day you shall offer a bull as a sin offering for atonement. Also you shall offer a sin offering for the altar, when you make atonement for it, and shall anoint it, to consecrate it.

Exodus 29:36

"On the tenth day of this seventh month is the day of atonement; it shall be for you a time of holy convocation, and you shall afflict yourselves and present an offering by fire to the Lord.

Leviticus 23:27

And burn the whole ram upon the altar; it is a burnt offering to the Lord; it is a pleasing odor, an offering by fire to the Lord.

Exodus 29:18

He shall tear it by its wings, but shall not divide it asunder. And the priest shall burn it on the altar, upon the wood that is on the fire; it is a burnt offering, an offering by fire, a pleasing odor to the Lord.

Leviticus 1:17

God Does Not Delight In Burnt Offerings

For in the day that I brought them out of the land of Egypt, I did not speak to your fathers or command them concerning burnt offerings and sacrifices.

Jeremiah 7:22

To what purpose does frankincense come to me from Sheba, or sweet can from a distant land? Your burnt offerings are not acceptable, nor your sacrifices pleasing to me.

Jeremiah 6:20

Do I eat the flesh of bulls, or drink the blood of goats? Offer to God a sacrifice of thanksgiving, and pay your vows to the Most High.

Psalms 50:13, 14

Bring no more vain offerings; incense is an abomination to me, New moon and Sabbath and the calling of assemblies -- I cannot endure iniquity and solemn assembly... What to me is the multitude of your sacrifices? says the Lord; I have had enough of burnt offerings of rams and the fat of fed beasts; I do not delight in the blood of bulls or of lambs, or of he-goats. When you come to appear before me, who requires of you this trampling of my courts.

Isaiah 1:13, 11, 12

God Approves Of Human Sacrifice

The king took the two sons of Rizpah the daughter of Aiah, whom she bore to Saul, Armoni and Mephibosheth; and the five sons of Merab the daughter of Saul, whom she bore to Adriel the son of Barzillai the Meholathite; and he gave them into the hands of the Gibeonites, and they hanged them on the mountain before the Lord, and the seven of them perished together. They were put to death in the first days of harvest, at the beginning of barley harvest... And they buried the bones of Saul and his son Jonathan in the land of Benjamin in Zela, in the tomb of Kish his father; and they did all that the king commanded. And after that God heeded supplications for the land.

2 Samuel 21:8, 9, 14

He said, "Take your son, your only son Isaac, whom you love, and go to the land of Moriah and offer him there as a burnt offering upon one of the mountains of which I shall tell you."

Genesis 22:2

And Jephthah made a vow to the Lord, and said, "If thou wilt give the Ammonites into my hand, then whoever comes forth from the doors of my house to meet me, when I return victorious from the Ammonites, shall be the Lord's and I will offer him up for a burnt offering." So Jephthah crossed over to the Ammonites to fight against them; and the Lord gave them into his hand... Then Jephthah came to his home at Mizpah; and behold, his daughter came out to meet him with timbrels and with dances; she was his only child; beside her he had neither son nor daughter... And he said, "Go." And he sent her away for two months; and she departed, she and her companions, and bewailed her virginity upon the mountains. And at the end of two months, she returned to her father, who did with her according to his vow which he had made. She had never known a man. And it became a custom in Israel.

Judges 11:30, 31,
32, 34, 38, 39

God Does Not Approve Of Human Sacrifice

Take heed that you be not ensnared to follow them, after they have been destroyed before you, and that you do not inquire about their gods, saying, 'How did these nations serve their gods? - that I also may do likewise. You shall not do so to the Lord your God; for every abominable thing which the Lord hates they have done for their gods; for they even burn their sons and their daughters in the fire to their gods.

Deuteronomy 12:30, 31

God is Unkind

And I will dash them one against another, fathers and sons together, says the Lord. I will not pity or spare or have compassion, that I should not destroy them.

Jeremiah 13:14

And you shall destroy all the peoples that the Lord your God will give over to you, your eye shall not pity them; neither shall you serve their gods, for that would be a snare to you.

Deuteronomy 7:16

Thus says the lord of hosts, 'I will punish what Amalek did to Israel in opposing them on the way, when they came up out of Egypt. Now go and smite Amalek, and utterly destroy all that they have; do not spare them, but kill both man and woman, infant, and suckling, ox, and sheep, camel and ass.

1 Samuel 15:2, 3

And watch; if it goes up on the way to its own land, to Bethshemesh, then it is he who had done us this great harm; but if not, then we shall know that it is not his hand that struck us, it happened to us by chance."

1 Samuel 6:19

For the Lord your God is a devouring fire, a jealous God.

Deuteronomy 4:24

God is Kind

for he does not willingly afflict or grieve the sons of men.

Lamentations 3:33

O give thanks to the Lord, for he is good; for his steadfast love endures for ever!

1 Chronicles 16:34

For I have no pleasure in the death of any one, says the Lord God; so turn, and live.

Ezekiel 18:32

The Lord is good to all, and his compassion is over all that he has made.

Psalms 145:9

Who desires all men to be saved and to come to the knowledge of the truth.

1 Timothy 2:4

So we know and believe the love God has for us. God is love, and he who abides in love abides in God, and God abides in him.

1 John 4:16

Good and upright is the Lord; therefore he instructs sinners in the way.

Psalms 25:8

God's Anger Endures 40 Years

And the Lord's anger was kindled against Israel, and he made them wander in the wilderness forty years, until all the generation that had done evil in the sight of the Lord was consumed.

Numbers 32:13

And the Lord said to Moses, "Take all the chiefs of the people, and hang them in the sun before the Lord, that the fierce anger of the Lord may turn away from Israel."

Numbers 25:4

117

On the mountains in the open country. Your wealth and all your treasures I will give for spoil as the price of your sin throughout all your territory.

Jeremiah 17:3

God's Anger Endures A Moment

The Lord is merciful and gracious, slow to anger and abounding in steadfast love.

Psalms 103:8

For his anger is but for a moment, and his favor is for a lifetime. Weeping may tarry for the night, but joy comes with the morning.

Psalms 30:5

God Is A Tempter

After these things God tested Abraham, and said to him, "Abraham!" And he said, "Here am I."

Genesis 22:1

Again the anger of the Lord was kindled against Israel, and he incited David against them, saying, "Go, number Israel and Judah."

2 Samuel 24:1

O Lord, thou hast deceived me, and I was deceived; thou art stronger than I, and thou hast prevailed. I have become a laughingstock all the day; ever one mock me.

Jeremiah 20:7

And lead us not into temptation, but deliver us from evil.

Matthew 6:13

God Is Not A Tempter

Let no one say when he is tempted. "I am tempted by God"' for God cannot be tempted with evil and he himself tempts no one;

James 1:13

God Can Not Tell A Lie

So that through two unchangeable things, in which it is impossible that God should prove false, we who have fled for refuge might have strong encouragement to seize the hope set before us.

Hebrews 6:18

118

God Lies Through Spirits

Therefore God sends upon them a strong delusion, to make them believe what is false.
2 Thessalonians 2:11

Now therefore behold, the lord has put a lying spirit in the mouth of all these your prophets; the Lord has spoken evil concerning you.
1 Kings 22:23

And if the prophet be deceived and speak a word, I, the Lord, have deceived that prophet, and I will stretch out my hand against him, and will destroy him from the midst of my people Israel.
Ezekiel 14:9

God Destroys Man

The Lord saw that the wickedness of man was great in the earth, and that every imagination of the thoughts of his heart was only evil continually... So the Lord said, "I will blot out man whom I have created from the face of the ground, man and beast and creeping things and birds of the air, for I am sorry that I have made them."
Genesis 6:5, 7

God Does Not Destroy Man

And when the Lord smelled the pleasing odor, the Lord said in his heart, "I will never again curse the ground because of man, for the imagination of man's heart is evil from his youth; neither will I ever again destroy every living creature as I have done.
Genesis 8:21

God Clearly Manifested In His Works

Ever since the creation of the world his invisible nature, namely, his eternal power and deity, has been clearly perceived in the things that have been made. So they are without excuse.
Romans 1:20

God Can Not Be Understood

"Can you find out the deep things of God? Can you find out the limit of the Almighty?
Job 11:7

Have you not known? Have you not heard? The Lord is the everlasting God, the Creator of the ends of the earth. He does not faint or grow weary, his understanding is unsearchable.

Isaiah 40:28

One God

You shall not go after other gods, of the gods of the peoples who are round about you.

Deuteronomy 6:14

Many Gods

Then God said, "Let us make man in our image, after our likeness; and let them have dominion over the fish of the sea, and over the birds of the air, and over the cattle, and over all the earth, and over every creeping thing that creeps upon the earth.

Genesis 1:26

Then the Lord God said, "Behold, the man has become like one of us, knowing good and evil; and now, lest he put forth his hand and take also of the tree of life, and eat and live for ever.

Genesis 3:22

And the Lord appeared to him by the oaks of Mamre, as he sat at the door of his tent in the heat of the day. He lifted up his eyes and looked, and behold, three men stood in front of him. When he saw them, he ran from the tent door to meet them, and bowed himself to the earth, and said, "My lord, if I have found favor in your sight, do not pass by your servant.

Genesis 18:1, 2, 3

And the Spirit is the witness, because the Spirit is the truth.

1 John 5:7

Robbery Commanded

And I will give this people favor in the sight of the Egyptians; and when you go, you shall not go empty, but each woman shall ask of her neighbor, and of her who sojourns in her house, jewelry of silver and of gold, and clothing, and you shall put them on your sons and on your daughters; thus you shall despoil the Egyptians.

Exodus 3:21, 22

The people of Israel had also done as Moses told them, for they had asked of the Egyptians jewelry of silver and of gold, and clothing; and the Lord had given the people favor in the sight of the Egyptians, so that they let them have what they asked. Thus they despoiled the Egyptians.

Exodus 12:35, 36

Robbery Not Commanded

"You shall not oppress your neighbor or rob him. The wages of a hired servant shall not remain with you all night until the morning."

Leviticus 19:13

You shall not steal.

Exodus 20:15

Bearing False Witness Is Permitted

But the woman had taken the two men and hidden them; and she said, "True, men came to me, but I did not know where they came from; and when the gate was to be closed, at dark, the men went out; where the men went I do not know; pursue them quickly, for you will overtake them." But she had brought them up to the roof, and hid them with the stalks of flax which she had laid in order on the roof.

Joshua 2:4, 5, 6

And in the same way was not also Rahab the harlot justified by works when she received the messengers and sent them out another way?

James 2:25

So the king of Egypt called the midwives, and said to them, "Why have you done this, and let the male children live?"... So God dealt well with the midwives; and the people multiplied and grew very strong.

Exodus 1:18, 20

Then a spirit came forward an stood before the Lord, saying, 'I will go forth, and will be a lying spirit in the mouth of all his prophets.' And he said, 'You are to entice him, and you shall succeed; go forth and do so.'

1 Kings 22:21, 22

Bearing False Witness Is Not Permitted

You shall not bear false witness against your neighbor.

Exodus 20:16

Lying lips are an abomination to the Lord, but those who act faithfully are his delight.

Proverbs 12:22

But as for the cowardly, the faithless, the polluted, as for murderers, fornicators, sorcerers, idolaters, and all liars, their lot shall be in the lake that burns with fire and sulphur, which is the second death."

Revelation 21:8

Animosity To The Edomites Is Permitted

He killed ten thousand Edomites in the Valley of Salt and took Sela by storm, and called it Jokthel, which is its name to this day... And he did what was right in the eyes of the Lord, yet not like David his father; he did in all things as Joash his father had done.

2 Kings 14:7, 3

Animosity To The Edomites Is Not Permitted

"You shall not abhor an Edomite, for he is your brother; you shall not abhor an Egyptian, because you were a sojourner in his land."

Deuteronomy 23:7

Killing Ordered

And he said to them, "Thus says the Lord God of Israel, 'Put every man his sword on his side, and go to and fro from gate to gate throughout the camp, and slay every man his brother, and every man his companion, and every man his neighbor.

Exodus 32:27

Killing Not Ordered

You shall not kill.

Exodus 20:13

No One Is Without Sin

If they sin against thee - for there is no man who does not sin - and thou art angry with them, and dost give them to an enemy, so that they are carried away captive to the land of the enemy, far off or near..

1 Kings 8:46

Who can say, "I have made my heart clean; I am pure from my sin"?

Proverbs 20:9

Surely there is not a righteous man on earth who does good and never sins.

Ecclesiastes 7:20

As it is written: "None is righteous, no, not one;

Romans 3:10

Certain Ones Are Without Sin

You know that he appeared to take away sins, and in him there is no sin. No one who abides in him sins; no one who sins has either seen him or known him... He who commits sin is of the devil; for the devil has sinned from the beginning. The reason the Son of God appeared was to destroy the works of the devil.

1 John 3:5, 6, 8

Resurrection Of The Dead

In a moment, in the twinkling of any eye, at the last trumpet. For the trumpet, will sound, and the dead will be raise imperishable, and we shall be changed.

1 Corinthians 15:52

And I saw the dead, great and small, standing before the throne, and books were opened. Also another book was opened, which is the book of life. And the dead were judged by what was written in the books, by what they had done.

Revelation 20:12, 13

But that the dead are raised, even Moses showed, in the passage about the bush, where he calls the Lord the God of Abraham and the God of Isaac and the God of Jacob.

Luke 20:37

For if the dead are not raised, then Christ has not been raised.

1 Corinthians 15:16

Resurrection Of The Dead Cannot Be Done

As the cloud fades and vanishes, so he who goes down to Sheol does not come up.

Job 7:9

For the living know that they will die, but the dead know nothing, and they have no more reward; but the memory of them is lost.

Ecclesiastics 9:5

They are dead, they will not live; they are shades, they will not arise; to that end thou hast visited them with destruction and wiped out all remembrance of them.

Isaiah 26:14

Reward & Punishment on Earth

If the righteous is requited on earth, how much more the wicked and the sinner!

Proverbs 11:31

Reward & Punishment In Next World

And the sea gave up the dead in it, Death and Hades gave up the dead in them, and all were judged by what they had done.

Revelation 20:13

For the Son of man is to come with his angels in the glory of his Father, and then he will repay every man for what he has done.

Matthew 16:27

For we must all appear before the judgment seat of Christ, so that each one may receive good or evil, according to what he has done in the body.

2 Corinthians 5:10

Earth Shall Be Destroyed

But the day of the Lord will come like a thief, and then the heavens will pass away with a loud noise, and the elements will be dissolved with fire, and the earth and the works that are upon it will be burned up.

2 Peter 3:10

They will perish, but thou remainest; they will all grow old like a garment.

Hebrews 1:11

Then I saw a great white throne and him who sat upon it; from his presence earth and sky fled away, and no place was found for them.

Revelation 20:11

Earth Shall Not Be Destroyed

A generation goes, and a generation comes, but the earth remains for ever.

Ecclesiastes 1:4

No Evil Shall Affect The Godly

No ill befalls the righteous, but the wicked are filled with trouble.
Proverbs 12:21

Now who is there to harm you if you are zealous for what is right?
1 Peter 3:13

Evil Shall Affect The Godly

For the Lord disciplines him whom he loves, and chastises every son whom he receives.
Hebrews 12:6

And the Lord said to Satan, "Have you considered my servant Job, that there is none like him on the earth, a blameless and upright man, who fears God and turns away from evil?" He still holds fast his integrity, although you moved me against him, to destroy him without cause."... So Satan went forth from the presence of the Lord, and afflicted Job with loathsome sores from the sole of his foot to the crown of his head.
Job 2:3, 7

Prosperity, Etc., For The Godly

No ill befalls the righteous, but the wicked are filled with trouble.
Proverbs 12:21

For the Lord loves justice; he will not forsake his saints. The righteous shall be preserved for ever, but the children of the wicked shall be cut off... The wicked watches the righteous, and seeks to slay him. The Lord will not abandon him to his power, or let him be condemned when he is brought to trial... Mark the blameless man, and behold the upright, for there is posterity for the man of peace.
Psalms 37:28, 32, 33, 37

The Lord was will Joseph, and he became a successful man; and he was in the house of his master the Egyptian.
Genesis 39:2

And the Lord blessed the latter days of Job more than his beginning; and he had fourteen thousand sheep, six thousand camels, a thousand yoke of oxen, and a thousand she-asses.
Job 43:12

They were stoned, they were sawn in two, they were killed with the sword; they went about in skins of sheep and goats, destitute, afflicted, ill-treated -- of whom the world was not worthy -- wandering over deserts and mountains, and in dens and caves of the earth

Hebrews 11:37, 38

I said to him, "Sir, you know." And he said to me, "These are they who have come out of the great tribulation; they have washed their robes and made them white in the blood of the Lamb."

Revelation 7:14

Indeed all who desire to live a godly life in Christ Jesus will be persecuted.

2 Timothy 3:12

You will be hated by all for my name's sake.

Luke 21:17

Prosperity A Blessing

I have been young, and now am old; yet I have not seen the righteous forsaken or his children begging bread.

Psalms 37:25

Praise the Lord! Blessed is the man who fears the Lord, who greatly delights in his commandments!... Wealth and riches are in his house; and his righteousness endures for ever.

Psalms 112:1, 3

In the house of the righteous there is much treasure, but trouble befalls the income of the wicked.

Proverbs 15:6

Prosperity A Curse

And he lifted up his eyes on his disciples, and said: "Blessed are you poor, for yours is the kingdom of God.

Luke 6:20

"Do not lay up for yourselves treasures on earth, where moth and rust consume and where thieves break in and steal... For where your treasure is, there will your heart be also.

Matthew 6:19, 21

The poor man died and was carried by the angels to Abraham's bosom. The rich man also died and was buried; and in Hades, being in torment, he lifted up his eyes, and saw Abraham far off and Lazarus in his bosom.

Luke 16:22, 23

Again I tell you, it is easier for a camel to go through the eye of a needle than for a rich man to enter the kingdom of God.

Matthew 19:24

"But woe to you that are rich, for you have received your consolation."

Luke 6:24

My Yoke Is Easy

Come to me, all who labor and are heavy laden, and I will give you rest... For my yoke is easy, and my burden is light.

Matthew 11:28, 30

My Yoke Is Not Easy

I have said this to you, that in me you may have peace. In the world you have tribulation; but be of good cheer, I have overcome the world.

John 16:33

While evil men and impostors will go on from bad to worse, deceivers and deceived.

2 Tim 3:12

For the Lord disciplines him whom he loves, and chastises every son whom he receives... If you are left without discipline, in which all have participated, then you are illegitimate children and not sons.

Heb 12:6, 8

Fruit Of The Spirit Is Love

But the fruit of the Spirit is love, joy, peace, patience, kindness, goodness,, faithfulness.

Galatians 5:22

When he came to Lehi, the Philistines came shouting to meet him; and the Spirit of the Lord came mightily upon him, and the ropes which were on his arms became as flax that has caught fire, and his bonds melted off his hands. And he found a fresh jawbone of an ass, and put out his hand and seized it, and with it he slew a thousand men.

Judges 15:14, 15

And on the morrow an evil spirit from God rushed upon Saul, and he raved within his house, while David was playing the lyre, as he did day by day. Saul had his spear in his hand; and Saul cast the spear, for he thought, "I will pin David to the wall." But David evaded him twice.

1 Samuel 18:10, 11

The Wicked Enjoy Longevity

Why do the wicked live, reach old age, and grow mighty in power? Their children are established in their presence?

Job 21:7, 8

From men by thy hand, O Lord, from men whose portion in life is of the world. May their belly be filled with what thou hast stored up for them; may their children have more than enough; may they leave something over to their babes.

Psalms 17:14

Though a sinner does evil a hundred times and prolongs his life, yet I know that it will be well with those who fear God, because they fear before him.

Ecclesiastes 8:12

No more shall there be in it an infant that lives but a few days, or an old man who does not fill out his days, for the child shall die a hundred years old, and the sinner a hundred years old shall be accursed.

Isaiah 65:20

The Wicked Will Not Enjoy Longevity

But it will not be well with the wicked, neither will he prolong his days like a shadow, because he does not fear before God.

Ecclesiastes 8:13

But thou, O God, wilt cast them down into the lowest pit; men of blood and treachery shall not live out half their days. But I will trust in thee.

Psalms 55:23

128

The fear of the Lord prolongs life, but the years of the wicked will be short.

Proverbs 10:27

They die in youth, and their life ends in shame.

Job 36:14

Be not wicked overmuch, neither be a fool; why should you die before your time?

Ecclesiastes 7:17

Poverty Considered A Blessing

And he lifted up his eyes on his disciples, and said: "Blessed are you poor, for yours is the kingdom of God."

Luke 6:20, 34

Listen, my beloved brethren. Has not God chosen those who are poor in the world to be rich in faith and heirs of the kingdom which he has promised to those who love him?

James 2:5

Riches Considered A Blessing

A rich man's wealth is his strong city; the poverty of the poor is their ruin.

Proverbs 10:15

If you return to the Almighty and humble yourself, if you remove unrighteousness far from your tents, if you lay gold in the dust, and gold of Ophir among the stones of the torrent bed.

Job 22:23, 24

And the Lord blessed the latter days of Job more than his beginning; and he had fourteen thousand sheep, six thousand camels, a thousand yoke of oxen and a thousand she-asses.

Job 42:12

Neither Considered A Blessing

Remove far from me falsehood and lying; give me neither poverty nor riches; feed me with the food that is needful for me.

Proverbs 30:8, 9

Wisdom Results In Happiness

Happy is the man who finds wisdom, and the man who gets understanding. for the gain from it is better than gain from silver and its profit better than gold... Her ways are ways of pleasantness, and all her paths are peace.

Proverbs 3:13, 14, 17

Wisdom A Source Of Vexation, Etc.

And I applied my mind to know wisdom and to know madness and folly. I perceived that this also is but a striving after wind. For in much wisdom is much vexation, and he who increases knowledge increases sorrow.

Ecclesiastes 1:17, 18

A Good Name A Blessing

A good name is better than precious ointment; and the day of death, than the day of birth.

Ecclesiastes 7:1

A good name is to be chosen rather than great riches, and favor is better than silver or gold.

Proverbs 22:1

A Good Name A Curse

"Woe to you, when all men speak well of you, for so their fathers did to the false prophets."

Luke 6:26

Mirth Commended

For everything there is a season, and a time for every matter under heaven... a time to weep, and a time to laugh.

Ecclesiastes 3:1, 4

And I commend enjoyment, for man has no good thing under the sun but to eat and drink and enjoy himself, for this will go with him in his toil through the days of life which God gives him under the sun.

Ecclesiastes 8:15

Mirth Condemned

"Woe to you that are full now, for you shall hunger. Woe to you that laugh now, for you shall morn and weep."

Luke 6:25

Sorrow is better than laughter, for by sadness of countenance the heart is made glad. The heart of the wise is in the house of mourning; but the heart of fools is in the house of mirth.

Ecclesiastes 7:3, 4

The Rod, A Remedy For Foolishness

Folly is bound up in the heart of a child, but the rod of discipline drives it far from him.

Proverbs 22:15

The Rod Is Not A Remedy For Foolishness

Crush a fool in a mortar with a pestle along with crushed grain, yet his folly will not depart from him.

Proverbs 27:22

Do Not Answer A Fool According To His Folly

Answer not a fool according to his folly, lest you be like him yourself.

Proverbs 26:4

Answer A Fool According To His Folly

Answer a fool according to his folly, lest he be wise in his own eyes.

Proverbs 26:5

Temptation Desired

Count it all joy, my brethren, when you meet various trials.

James 1:2

Temptation Is Not Desired

And lead us not into temptation, but deliver us from evil.

Matthew 6:13

Moses A Very Meek Man

Now the man Moses was very meek, more than all men that were on the face of the earth.

Numbers 12:3

Moses Was Vindictive

Moses said to them, "Have you let all the women live?... Now therefore, kill every male among the little ones, and kill every woman who has known man by lying with him.

Numbers 31:15, 17

Elijah Ascended To Heaven

And as they still went on and talked, behold, a chariot of fire and horses of fire separated the two of them. And Elijah went up by a whirlwind into heaven.

2 Kings 2:11

None But Christ Will Ascend To Heaven

No one has ascended into heaven but he who descended from heaven, the Son of man.

John 3:13

All Scripture Given By Inspiration

All scripture is inspired by God and profitable for teaching, for reproof, for correction, and for training in righteousness.

2 Timothy 3:16

Some Scripture Given By Inspiration

I say this by way of concession, not of command.

1 Corinthians 7:6

What I am saying I say not with the Lord's authority but as a fool, in this boastful confidence.

2 Corinthians 11:17

Conclusions

So we come at last to the end of our study of "The Good Book", which isn't quite as good as maybe you at first thought. The Bible is no more than a chronicle of deceit, duplicity and lies that has been and still is, forced on people as "the word of God". We hope that our efforts have not gone in vain. We hope that some of our readers will, at least, have a better understanding of what, in all actuality, is only myth, legend, and parable. If you want to read the Bible, then, by all means do so. We only want you to know from what it was derived.

It is up to you to accept or reject the facts presented here. We encourage each of you to read the relevant sources listed in the Bibliography and end-notes and come to your own conclusions. Again, it is not our intent to convert anyone to any other religion, only to present the truth "and the truth shall make you free".

> "Every compromise of the truthfulness of the Bible must at the same time be regarded as a compromise of its authority." [1]
>
> - F. F. Bruce

There comes a time in everyone's life when they have to decide whether or not to put aside the doctrines of childhood that are inconsistent with the reality of life as an adult. We would be doing ourselves, family and loved ones a grave injustice to cling blindly and irrationally to erroneous and misleading beliefs that contradict our sense of self, worth, and good sense.

Since no Christian church is likely to inform anyone of scientific discoveries that contradict published doctrines, we the authors feel there are a few things that everyone should know. In this vein, we offer the following, "parting shots":

During the 1840s "The American School" of Anthropology came out in favor of polygenesis as opposed to monogenesis. What this means is that Anthropologists feel that the human race must have descended from more than one set of parents, in contradiction to the biblical account of Adam and Eve.

Horace Bushnell, a distinguished theologian writing in the 1800s stated the following: **"The mythological stories of the gospels have a real value but are quite unworthy of credit as facts."** [2]

German scholarship during the 1800's brought an end to the myth that Moses was the author of the Pentateuch. The position that he had been was insupportable after 1849.[3]

> **"The modern interpretation of the Bible, for example, starts with the premise that everything in the Book of Genesis up to the construction of the Tower of Babel is quite simply a parable in which the authors were trying to make comprehensible the unfathomable workings of the Lord."** [4]
>
> — Barthel

Matthew Arnold, also a theologian, wrote the following in 1873:

> **"To understand the language of the Bible is fluid, passing, and literary, not rigid, fixed, and scientific is the first step to a right understanding of the Bible."** [5]

Even the founder of Calvinism warned against pushing literalism too far. **"Moses"**, he said, **"never meant to teach history."** [6]

If, as Mr. Bushnell states, **"the gospels are quite unworthy of credit as facts"** then the authority of the Bible as a historical foundation for Christian beliefs simply collapses!

The gospels create a myth of a man/god: precisely the approach to religion that we would expect from a primitive people like the early Hebrews.

Two books published five years apart by the eminent British scientist Sir John Lubbock point out the obscure and sometimes disgusting origins of chaste Victorian marriage customs.

1. *Prehistoric Times*, published in 1865
2. *The Origin of Civilization*, published in 1870

Rites and doctrines central to Christianity are disclosed as primitive survivals.

Baptism appears, in these books, to be just "one more purification ritual". The Eucharist becomes the widely used and ceremonial eating of a god. In the words of the author, Sir John, Christianity is "only the modified superstitions of barbarous ages".

134

Christianity, like all other great religions, amounts to only a "well meant approximation to some grander divine truth."

- Sir John Lubbock

The existence of a creation (humanity) that operates against the will of the Creator suggests to us that He is not all good. He is ready to reward some and punish others. If God were all powerful, wouldn't he be able to bring His creation in line with his purposes?

We know that someone is going to say that man has freewill and God lets man choose what he wants to do but the Bible says otherwise. Man does not have freewill.

"God has consigned all men to disobedience, that He may have mercy on all."

Romans 11:32

- We have shown that the morality of Christianity in the form of Jesus is inferior to, and in all fact, was copied from the ancient philosophies that preceded him.

- How can any reasonable and sane person believe in a God that abandons His Creation for long periods of time and then after neglecting them, decides to exterminate them and start over. This is not a book of divine anything.

- In the original Scriptures, the one foretold was to be "a great prince" and a "leader of nations and armies". Christ was neither of these.

- "The Good Book" is not good and anyone who would depend on it is, at the very least, misguided.

- The Bible is not "inspired" or God-given. It is plagiarism, corrupted to its own ends.

"Just as the charlatans of the cults take advantage of a simpleton's lack of education to lead him around by the nose, so with the Christian teachers." [7]

- Celsus

"The Bible is a dangerous, uncivilized, abrasive, raw, complicated, aggressive, scandalous, and offensive work."

- Schaffer

"As men look back upon nations in the olden time, and know that amid their fondest convictions they were in profound error . . . that their gods were myths, their histories half fables, and their theology mere fiction, so now and then it came back to him with ghastly distinctness that a time would come when men would look back on his generation in the same manner."

Henry Ward Beecher
"Norwood" (1868)

Appendix - "A"

Players in the Biblical Drama

Albigenses:
(c. 1080) Offshoot of Manicheism, had their own pastors, bishops, and councils. One of the most active of the heretical, Christian sects. Their goal was to make Jerusalem, not Rome, the Papal Seat.

Cathari:
Another of the heresies. Wanted to restore the Christianity of the apostles. (What did they know that we don't?) Named "the Apostolic", they predicted the downfall of the Papacy. Exterminated in a "crusade" by Clement V. **Anyone that opposed the church was eliminated, the church would stand no opposition.**

Celsus:
(c.200) Aulus Cornelius Celsus, Patrician Roman Scholar, wrote at length on medicine, philosophy, and religion.

Diocletian:
(c. 280 CE) Gaius Aurelius Valarius Diocletianus, a Roman Emperor who helped to create many Christian Saints through martyrdom.

Docetism:
Gnostic heresy that opposed a literal belief in Christ.

Epiphanius:
A father of the church, said to be friend of St. Jerome.

Eusebius:
Bishop of Caesarea under Constantine I, voluminous writer and known "corrector" of Biblical texts. Claimed that the Essenes were Christians and their writings "Our gospels and epistles."

Ingersoll:
(1833-1899) Robert Ingersoll, American lawyer and lecturer, outspoken critic of the Bible. Served as attorney General for State of Illinois.

Irenaeus:
Bishop of Lyons during 2nd century.

Jones:
Maurice Jones, Author of "The New Testament in the Twentieth Century," written in 1934.

Manicheans:
Founded by Mani, (c. 242) a Persian prophet. St Augustine claimed membership for ten years before becoming "orthodox" and writing against them. Manichaeism was a synthesis of Gnostic, Buddhist, and Zoroastrian philosophy with Christianity. "If the blood of the martyrs were really the seed of the Church, Manichaeism would now be the dominant religion of Europe." Written by Henry Charles Lea, quoted in Campbell, 496.

Origen:
(c. 185-254 CE) Origenes Adamantius was his full name. He was an Egyptian writing in Greek, exerted powerful influence for early church.

Philo Judaeus:
(c. 30 BCE-40 CE) Jewish Philosopher living in Alexandria, author of Biblical commentaries and histories.

Pliny:
(c. 22-79 CE) "The Elder," Procurator of Spain and prolific author, never mentions Christ.

Pliny:
(c. 62-110 CE) "The Younger," Governor of Bythonia, Christ is unknown to him.

Porphy:
(c. 234-305 CE) Neoplatonist philosopher, scholar, and writer. Biographer of Plotinus, most of his work was burned by the church.

Seneca:
Brother of the Proconsul of Achaia, Author of "Questionum Naturalium".

St Augustine:
(c. 354-430 CE) "Founder of Christian Theology," wrote "The City of God" to answer the question: Why did Rome survive for centuries under paganism and die when it turned to Christianity?

St. John Chrysostom:
(c.550) Christian orator, nicknamed "Golden-mouthed John" because of his skill.

Stanton:
(1815-1902) Elizabeth Cady Stanton, Associate of Susan B. Anthony; leader of Woman's Rights, opponent of Bible as suppressive of Woman's Rights

Tacitus:
(c. 56-120 CE) Cornelius Tacitus, Roman historian and rhetorician.

Tertullian:
(c. 155-220 CE) His full name was Quintus Septimius Florens Tertullianus. Early church advocate, born of Pagan parents.

Tyndale:
(c. 1494-1536) William Tyndale was an English ecclesiastical reformer. Translator of the first English language Bibles, executed in Brussels.

Waldenses:
A heretical sect led by Peter Waldo in southern France. Preached simplicity and poverty in imitation of Christ.

Wellhausen:
(1844-1918) Julius Wellhausen, German Biblical scholar and opponent.

Appendix - "B"

Players in the Mythological Drama

Abraham:
"Father Braham", a fictional character based on Brahama, the patriarchal god of India, adapted as the Patriarch of Judaism.

Adam:
Fictional first man, became "fool" of the Tarot, an archetype of primitive man.

Eve:
Name given to the wife of Adam, mythological mother of the human race. Her name means "life" in the original myths.

Gospel of Mary:
An earlier "Gnostic" gospel, at one time included in the New Testament, later eliminated as unfit by misogynic priests.

Jonah:
Mythological character "swallowed" by whale.

Mahabharata:
Epic East Indian poem, included both historical and legendary material, included Bhagavad-Gita.

Mammon:
Medieval demon of riches, created in response to Luke 16:13, "you cannot serve God and Mammon". The temples of The Goddess were far richer than those of the Hebrew Yahveh, hence the quotation.

Marduk:
Babylonian Patriarchal deity that overcame "the Mother" Tiamat, strongly influenced Patriarchal Hebrews. Inheritor of the "sacred tablets" of the law from the Goddess which became the tablets upon which Yahweh wrote "His" laws - the ten commandments.

Mari:

The "Mary" of the Hindus, Mother of the Hindu savior. Her Latin name was Maria, "the seas" (oceans) of life. Model for Biblical Mary.

Mithra:

Persian savior, leading rival to Christianity in Roman Empire c. 300 CE. Born on the 25th of December also. St. Augustine said that priests of Mithra worshiped same deity as he.

Moses:

Fictional author of the first five books of the bible.

Protoevangelium:

The "Revelation of St. James," included in earlier Bibles, later eliminated.

St. Thomas:

Hellenized name of the god Tammuz, traditional dying savior of the Jerusalem Cult who was supplanted by Christ. Tammuz then became doubting Thomas, challenger of the Christ.

Tiamat:

Babylonian "Mother of the Universe", overthrown by male divinity, Marduk. Beginning of male domination of women.

Bibliography

1. *Deceptions and Myths in the Bible*, Graham, Citadel Press, 1991.

2. *When God was a Woman*, Stone, Harper Books, 1975.

3. *The Great Cosmic Mother*, Sjoo & Mor, Harcort Brace Publishers, 1991.

4. *Occidental Mythology*, Campbell, Penguin Books, 1991.

5. *Isis Unveiled*, Volumes 1 & 2, Blavatsky, Theosophical Publishing Co., 1888.

6. *The Secret Doctrine*, Volumes 1 & 2, Blavatsky, Theosophical Publishing Co.,1888.

7. *Primitive Mythology*, Campbell, Penguin Books, 1991.

8. *The Christians as the Romans Saw Them*, Wilkensen, Yale University Press, 1984.

9. *The Story of Civilization*, Vol 3, Durant, Simon and Shuster, 1965.

10. *Transformation of Myths Through Time*, Campbell, Harper and Row Publishers, 1990.

11. *The Power of Myth*, Campbell/Moyers, Doubleday Publishers, 1988.

12. *Great Classical Myths*, Godolphin Ed., Random House Publishers, 1964.

13. *Creative Mythology*, Campbell, Penguin Books, 1991.

14. *On The True Doctrine*, Celsus, Translation by Jos. Hoffmann, Oxford University Press, 1988.

15. *The Once and Future Goddess*, Gadon, Harper and Row Publishers, 1989.

16. *Secret Societies of All Ages and Countries*, Hecklthorn, Volume 1 & 2, University Books, 1977.

17. *Great Events From History*, Magill Ed., Vol 1, Salem Press, 1972.

18. *The Gilgamesh Epic and Old Testament Parallels*, Heidel, University of Chicago Press, 1949.

19. *History Begins at Sumer*, Kramer, Thames and Hudson, 1961.

20. *Archeology and the Bible*, Barton, American Sunday School Union, 1937.

21. *Ancient Near Eastern Texts Relating to the Old Testament*, Pritchard, Princeton University Press, 1950.

22. *Hebrew Origins*, Meek, Harper & Row, 1960.

23. *The Babylonian Genesis*, Heidel, University of Chicago Press, 1951.

24. *The Age of Reason*, Paine, Buccaneer Books, 1976.

25. *The Origin of the Bible*, Comfort, ed., Tyndale House Publishers, 1992.

26. *Pagans and Christians*, Fox, Knopf Publishers Inc., 1987.

27. *Without God-Without Creed*, Turner, John Hopkins University Press, 1985.

28. *Bertrand Russell on God and Religion*, Seckel, ed., Prometheus Books, 1986.

29. *Thomas Paine*, Wilson and Ricketson, G.K. Hall, 1978.

30. *What is Religion?*, Haught, Paulist Press, 1990.

31. *Difficulties & Alleged Errors in The Bible*, Torry, Bible Institute Colportage Assn., 1906.

32. *Woman's Encyclopedia of Myth's and Secrets*, Walker, Harper and Row, 1983.

33. *The Book of The Goddess - Past & Present*, Olson, ed., Crossroad Publishing, 1989.

34. *What the Bible Really Says*, Barthel, Translation by Mark Howson, Quill, 1983.

35. *Secret Teachings of All Ages*, Hall, Philosophical Research Society, 1977.

36. *Pagan Christs*, Robertson, University Books, 1967.

37. *The Story of Philosophy*, Durant, Simon and Shuster, 1953.

38. *The Dead Sea Scrolls*, Burrows, Viking Press, 1955.

39. *More Light on the Dead Sea Scrolls*, Burrows, Viking Press, 1958.

40. *A History of Philosophical Systems*, Ferm, ed., The Philosophy Library, 1950. (Vergilius Ferm presents a series of Papers from colleagues, in various schools of Philosophy, Including, but not limited to "Ancient Jewish Philosophy" by Samuel S. Cohon, Professor of Jewish Theology, Hebrew Union College; "Early Christian Philosophy" by Vergilius Ferm, Compton Professor and Head of the Dept of Philosophy, College of Wooster).

41. *A History of the Warfare of Science with Theology* (vol. 1 and 2), White, George Braziller, 1955

42. *The Golden Ass*, Apuleius, Translation by Robert Graves, Pocketbooks, 1951

Notes

Preface:
1. Sjoo & Mor, 311
2. Campbell, 53

Chapter One:
1. Durant, 202
2. Howson, 11
3. Ibid: 1982 stats.
4. Archeology has proven that the Bible can not be accepted as history.
5. Comfort, 95
6. Wilkensen, 13
7. Ibid,12
8. Campbell, Masks of God, Vol III, 126
9. Wilkensen, 12
10. Ibid, 11
11. Ibid, 11
12. Ibid, 12
13. Paine, 294
14. Sjoo & Mor, 332-333
15. For a fuller discussion of the 'earlier' Goddess traditions see books by the following authors: Gadon, Stone, Sjoo & Mor, Olsen, or the "Masks" Series by Jos. Campbell.

Chapter Two:
1. White, vol III, 328
2. Campbell, "Masks," vol III, 95-100
3. Howson, 156
4. Campbell,
5. Ferm, 57

6. Hoffman, 36
7. Heidel, 63
8. Howson, 33
9. Meek, 25
10. Gadon, 16
11. Graham, 78
12. Heidel, 40
13. Pritchard, 67
14. Ferm, 63
15. Meek, 35
16. Barton, 77
17. Ferm, 62
18. Heidel, 51
19. Pritchard, 91
20. Howson, 257
21. Ferm, 63

Chapter Three:
1. Comfort, 156
2. For description of this and other heresies see Appendix "A"
3. Blavatsky, 477
4. Hoffman, 94
5. Ibid, 344
6. Campbell, "Masks" vol 3, 334
7. Secret Doctrine, 541-542
8. Paine, 331
9. Graham, 409

Chapter Four:
1. Burrows, 43
2. Hoffman, 53
3. Blavatsky, 33-36
4. Burrows, 43
5. Ibid, 44
6. Howson, 119

7. Blavatsky, 249
8. Graham, 451
9. Graham, 288
10. Ibid, 445
11. Ibid, 447
12. Ibid
13. Torry, 236
14. Burrows, 41
15. Ibid, 40
16. Campbell, 110

Chapter Five:
1. Blavatsky, 124
2. Graham, 466
3. Walker 787

Chapter Six:
1. Blavatsky, 250
2. Sjoo & Mor, 317
3. Paine, 296

Chapter Seven:
1. Blavatsky, 501
2. Fox, 125
3. Walker, 551
4. White, 1, 337
5. Walker, 223
6. Ibid, 227

Chapter Eight:
1. Sjoo & Mor, 292
2. Ibid
3. Ibid
4. Ibid
5. Ibid
6. Stone, 224
7. Ibid, 226
8. Ibid, 224
9. Torry, 212
10. Stone, ix
11. Sjoo & Mor, 204

Chapter Nine:
1. Durant, 432
2. Graham, 449
3. Ibid
4. Ibid, 451

Conclusions:
1. Comfort, 121
2. Haught, 286
3. White, 227
4. Howson, 57
5. White, 235
6. Torry, 151
7. Hoffman, 54
